Chetna Makan

CLASSIC
INDIAN
RECIPES

Chetna Makan

CLASSIC INDIAN RECIPES

75 signature dishes

hamlyn

First published in Great Britain in 2025
by Hamlyn, an imprint of
Octopus Publishing Group Ltd
Carmelite House
50 Victoria Embankment
London EC4Y 0DZ
www.octopusbooks.co.uk

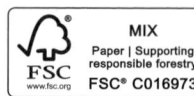

An Hachette UK Company
www.hachette.co.uk

The authorised representative in the EEA is Hachette Ireland,
8 Castlecourt Centre, Castleknock Road,
Castleknock, Dublin 15, D15 YF6A, Ireland

Some of this material previously appeared in *Chetna's 30 Minute Indian*, *Chai, Chaat & Chutney*, *Chetna's Indian Feasts*, *Chetna's Healthy Indian* and *Chetna's Healthy Indian Vegetarian*.

Copyright © Octopus Publishing Group Ltd 2025
Text copyright © Chetna Makan 2025

ISBN 978-0-600-63888-9

A CIP catalogue record for this book is available from the British Library

Printed and bound in China

10 9 8 7 6 5 4 3 2 1

Publisher: Lucy Pessell
Designer: Isobel Platt
Photographer: Nassima Rothacker
Editor: Feyi Oyesanya
Assistant Editor: Samina Rahman
Production Manager: Allison Gonsalves

Both metric and imperial measurements are given for the recipes.
Use one set of measures only, not a mixture of both.

Ovens should be preheated to the specified temperature. If using a fan-assisted oven, follow the manufacturer's instructions for adjusting the time and temperature. Grills should also be preheated.

This books includes dishes made with nuts and nut derivatives. It is advisable for those with known allergic reactions to nuts and nut derivatives and those who may be potentially vulnerable to these allergies, such as pregnant and nursing mothers, invalids, the elderly, babies and children, to avoid dishes made with nuts and nut oils. It is also prudent to check the labels of preprepared ingredients for the possible inclusion of nut derivatives.

The Department of Health advises that eggs should not be consumed raw. This book contains some dishes made with raw or lightly cooked eggs. It is prudent for more vulnerable people such as pregnant and nursing mothers, invalids, the elderly, babies and young children to avoid uncooked or lightly cooked dishes made with eggs.

Meat and poultry should be cooked thoroughly. To test if poultry is cooked, pierce the flesh through the thickest part with a skewer or fork – the juices should run clear, never pink or red.

CONTENTS

Introduction 6

Chaat 8

Vegetables 30

Meat & Fish 58

Dals 88

Rice & Breads 102

Chutneys & Sides 122

Sweet Things 134

Index 156

Glossary of Terms 160

INTRODUCTION

To try and summarize Indian cuisine is not an easy task. India is a large, diverse country and the food varies from region to region. Northern India, for example, is known as India's bread basket, and its dishes are often accompanied by roti or paratha. In South India, coconut trees are abundant, so coconut is often a key ingredient here. Some regions, such as the state of Gujarat, are predominantly vegetarian due to religious reasons, while coastal India is known for its unique seafood dishes. From the mouthwatering chaat of Jabalpur (the small town in central India where I grew up) to the dosa and sambhar of South India, India's food culture is both delicious and diverse.

And India's food culture doesn't stop in India – look no further than the now-traditional British Friday night curry, a concept that was totally new to me when I moved to the UK many years ago but one that I have whole-heartedly embraced.

A common thread in Indian cuisine is the emphasis on delicious, fresh ingredients. Growing up, my mum would buy fresh veg from the street vendor who came calling to our road every morning and choose her dishes for the day based on what he was selling. If she bought enough vegetables, he would throw in some green chillies and a lime for free, so you can imagine how fresh our meals were.

Staple ingredients include rice, wholewheat flour and a wide variety of lentils and pulses, and of course you'll find these in many of the recipes throughout this book. Popular spices include cardamom, cumin, turmeric, ginger, coriander and the favoured spice mix garam masala.

Narrowing down 75 recipes was no mean feat, but I have selected recipes that reflect various key elements of Indian cuisine, from street food staples and sweet treats to delectable dals and flavourful curries. Whether you are entertaining friends and family or rustling up a simple midweek meal, I hope you will find plenty to enjoy in this book.

The Indian menu

Chaat (sour and spicy street food snacks): Street food is a huge and important part of India's food culture. Most street food is freshly prepared to order, served very quickly and, best of all, extremely cheap. My family's street food favourites were the chaat – bhel puri, pani puri and papdi chaat. The stall that made the best chaat in Jabalpur still exists! The next generation of stallholders gradually learned the tricks of the trade, so whenever I visit my parents, I make sure to go there and enjoy some more of what I consider to be the best chaat I've ever tasted.

Vegetarian dishes: I grew up in India, so vegetarianism is not new to me. My dad is vegetarian and so are many of my friends and relatives. Many of my go-to recipes are vegetarian and contain lots of fresh, seasonal vegetables, which are not only low in fat but packed full of nutrients and fibre, which we all know are good for you.

Meat and fish: Fish is a great source of protein and contains lots of minerals, including calcium and much more, making it a very healthy choice. Similarly, chicken is not just delicious, but brilliant for all its protein, minerals and vitamins. I've included a variety of flavour-packed yet super-simple curries.

Dals: I tend to cook a lot with lentils – a great source of protein, fibre, vitamins and much more. They are easy to store and cook, so are brilliant for midweek meals. But the best part, as far as I'm concerned, is the huge variety of lentils there is to choose from. Each type has a unique texture and flavour; if I specify a type of lentil in a recipe and you choose another one, the result will not be as intended. Don't worry – it can still taste great, but factors such as the flavour, texture and cooking time will need to change. So please do try to use the specified lentils in each recipe to get the best results.

Rice and breads: Of course, a curry needs to be enjoyed with rice or roti. These are a key part of any Indian meal. The rice recipes here are varied and many work perfectly as meals on their own, such as Peanut, Coriander and Lemon Rice or Aubergine and Potato Rice. The flatbreads are also brilliant and can be served with any of the curries in this book.

Chutneys and sides: All my friends know how much I love chutney and pickles! I believe adding a dollop of good chutney to your meal can make it extraordinary. The ingredients used in them are super-healthy too. Turn a simple flatbread into a feast of a snack with some pickle, make your lentils a little more special with a chutney or elevate your curry with a raita.

Sweet things: If you're someone who needs to finish meals with a little something sweet, that's exactly what you'll find here. Desserts are an important part of Indian cuisine, irresistibly sweet and rich with flavour. The desserts and treats here are mostly bite-size – ideal for enjoying in moderation. Whether it's a delicious Almond Halwa or a refreshing glass of Mango Lassi, these sweet treats are the perfect finishing touch for any meal.

CHAAT

Dahi Puri

SERVES 4
1 medium potato,
  peeled, boiled and
  cooled
50 ml (2 fl oz) water
200 ml (7 fl oz) natural
  yogurt
24 puris (pani puri)
tamarind jaggery
  chutney, to taste
coriander yogurt
  chutney, to taste
¼ teaspoon salt
¼ teaspoon chilli
  powder
¼ teaspoon chaat
  masala
nylon sev (gram flour
  noodles), to taste

This dahi puri is a version of the popular snack pani puri, but instead of spicy water, the puri is filled with yogurt before being topped with a medley of flavours. Puris are readily available in Asian shops by the name of pani puri, as is 'nylon' sev, which is just a quirky name for superfine sev, a crunchy snack made with gram (besan/chickpea) flour. You can prepare all the elements beforehand, but put the dish together just before serving so that it retains its satisfying crispiness.

1 Break up the boiled potato roughly by hand.

2 Whisk the measured water and yogurt in a bowl until the mixture is smooth.

3 When you are ready to serve, place the puris on a dish and, using your thumb, gently break the top of each one to make a small opening. Load up each puri with a little of the potato, then add a good tablespoon or more of the yogurt on top. Now drizzle over some of the tamarind and coriander chutneys. Sprinkle the salt, chilli powder and chaat masala on top, then scatter the sev over the puris to finish. Serve immediately.

Crispy Paneer Cubes

SERVES 2
2 tablespoons gram
flour (besan)
70 ml (2½ fl oz)
natural yogurt
¼ teaspoon salt
1 teaspoon kashmiri
chilli powder
1 teaspoon kasuri
methi (dried
fenugreek leaves)
½ teaspoon amchur
(mango powder)
½ teaspoon garam
masala
½ teaspoon ground
cumin
200 g (7 oz) paneer,
cut into 2.5 cm
(1 inch) cubes
sunflower oil, for
shallow-frying

Snack, light meal, side or starter – I don't know how to categorize this dish. In India, you would serve it as a snack with some chai or even as a starter, however heavy the meal to follow (there is always room for fried paneer). The spiced yogurt is a great marinade, with the addition of gram flour ensuring that it sticks to the paneer. Toasting the flour is important, as it eliminates the raw taste, resulting in a delicious and crisp paneer. Serve with some coriander chutney.

1 Heat a frying pan, add the flour and toast over a low heat for about 2 minutes until it starts to change colour, stirring constantly.

2 Put the toasted flour into a bowl with the yogurt, salt and spices and mix together well. Add the paneer cubes and gently turn in the marinade until well coated.

3 Heat enough oil for shallow-frying in a frying pan. Carefully add the paneer to the hot oil and cook over a medium–high heat for 1–2 minutes, turning halfway through, until golden and crispy. Serve warm.

Cheesy Potato Balls

MAKES 8

2 potatoes, peeled and
  cut into 1 cm
  (½ inch) pieces
1 tablespoon sunflower
  oil, plus extra for
  deep-frying
1 green chilli, finely
  chopped
10 fresh curry leaves,
  finely chopped
½ teaspoon black
  mustard seeds
½ teaspoon salt
½ teaspoon chilli
  powder
½ teaspoon ground
  turmeric
1 tablespoon water
30 g (1 oz) Cheddar
  cheese, cut into
  small cubes

FOR THE BATTER

100 g (3½ oz) gram
  flour (besan)
½ teaspoon salt
½ teaspoon chilli
  powder
½ teaspoon ground
  turmeric
about 120 ml
  (4 fl oz) water

This widely loved snack in India, which is famed in Mumbai as batata vada, is customarily sold in a soft bun with a garlic and chilli chutney. Its popularity has spread and it's now available in many Indian restaurants worldwide. Where I come from, these delicious potato balls are called alu banda and are sold in small shops and street stalls in the mornings for breakfast with chai. So why not serve this with some coriander chutney and piping hot masala chai?

1   Put the potato pieces in a pan and cover with water. Bring to the boil and cook for 5 minutes until tender. Drain and set aside.

2   Heat the 1 tablespoon of oil in a pan and add the green chilli, curry leaves and mustard seeds. Once they start to sizzle, stir in the salt and ground spices and cook over a low heat for a few seconds. Add the measured water and the cooked potatoes and mix well, then leave to cool while you make the batter.

3   Mix together all the batter ingredients except the water in a bowl. Then gradually whisk in enough of the water to make a smooth batter with a coating consistency.

4   Divide the potato mixture into 8 portions and form each into a ball about the size of a lime. Push a cube of cheese into the centre of each potato ball and mould the potato mixture back around it to seal it in.

5   Heat enough oil for deep-frying in a deep-fat fryer or deep, heavy-based pan (ensuring the pan is no more than one-third full) to 180°C (350°F). Line a plate with kitchen paper. Dip one potato ball at a time into the batter and then carefully add to the hot oil. Deep-fry, in small batches, for a minute on each side until golden. Transfer to the paper-lined plate to absorb the excess oil while you fry the remaining balls. Serve warm.

Bhakarwadi

MAKES 60
sunflower oil, for
deep-frying

FOR THE PASTRY
150 g (5 ½ oz) plain
flour
50 g (1 ¾ oz) gram flour
(besan)
¼ teaspoon salt
¼ teaspoon ground
turmeric
about 100 ml
(3 ½ fl oz) water

FOR THE FILLING
25 g (1 oz) sesame seeds
25 g (1 oz) white
poppy seeds
25 g (1 oz) desiccated
coconut
1 teaspoon fennel
seeds
1 teaspoon sunflower
oil
1 teaspoon finely
chopped ginger
1 tablespoon gram
flour (besan)
½ teaspoon salt
½ teaspoon chilli
powder
1 ½ teaspoon
granulated sugar
1 teaspoon ground
coriander
1 teaspoon ground
cumin

These tiny sweet-savoury snacks are found at most of the tea stalls in Mumbai. The pastry is filled with beautiful spices and fried to give a crisp finish. Stored in an airtight box, they will keep you going for days – that is, if they last that long!

1 To make the pastry, put the flours in a bowl with the salt and turmeric. Slowly mix in just enough of the measured water (or a little more, if necessary) to form a soft dough. Knead for 2 minutes, then cover the bowl with clingfilm and leave to rest for 15–20 minutes.

2 To make the filling, toast the sesame seeds in a dry pan over a low heat for 2 minutes, without letting them change colour. Tip the seeds into a bowl. Repeat with the poppy seeds, then with the coconut, then the fennel seeds. Add the remaining filling ingredients to the seeds and coconut and mix well.

3 Divide the dough into 4 portions. Working with each portion in turn, roll it out into a thin circle with a diameter of roughly 22–23 cm (8½–9 inches). Using a pastry brush, dampen the pastry circle with water. Sprinkle a quarter of the filling mixture over it and press down slightly. Roll up the circle like a Swiss roll, then cut crossways into pieces with a thickness of about 15 mm (⅝ inch).

4 Fill a deep-fat fryer or deep, heavy-based saucepan with enough oil for deep-frying and heat it to 170–180°C (340–350°F). Line a plate with some kitchen paper. Working in batches, fry the bhakarwadi for about 2 minutes on each side, until golden brown. Transfer to the paper-lined plate to drain excess oil. Serve hot or cold.

Smashed Alu Tikki

MAKES 8
4 medium potatoes,
  peeled and cut into
  quarters
¾ teaspoon salt
¾ teaspoon chilli
  powder
4 tablespoons
  cornflour
8 tablespoons
  sunflower oil

TO SERVE
150 ml (¼ pint)
  natural yogurt
50 ml (2 fl oz) water
pinch of salt
pinch of chilli powder
pinch of chaat masala
coriander yogurt
  chutney, to taste
tamarind jaggery
  chutney, to taste

Alu tikki is one of the most popular chaats in India and beyond, and it's certainly high up there on my list, too. Often on street corners you can find vendors selling this tikki chaat. They semi-prepare the potato cutlets, half-cooking them in small balls. As soon as you place an order, they turn up the heat, squash the tikkis and fry them until crispy and golden. I usually prepare this dish as a chaat, but you can serve the tikkis without the toppings as a snack or a party canapé.

1 Cook the potatoes in a saucepan of boiling water until cooked through and soft. Drain, set aside in a bowl until cool enough to handle, then mash them with a potato masher. Now add the salt, chilli powder and cornflour to the mash and mix it all well. Divide the mixture into 8 portions and shape them into balls.

2 Heat 2 tablespoons of the oil in a frying pan over a low heat. Add 4 potato balls and cook for 2 minutes on each side until lightly golden. Now add 2 more tablespoons of oil to the pan and, using the back of a large metal or wooden spoon, flatten the balls into flat cakes. Increase the heat to medium and cook for 2 minutes on each side until deep golden brown. Repeat with the remaining 4 potato balls to complete frying the tikkis.

3 Put the yogurt into a bowl, add the measured water and whisk until the mixture is smooth.

4 Place the tikkis on a serving plate and drizzle over the yogurt. Sprinkle the salt, chilli powder and chaat masala on top. Now drizzle over the chutneys and serve immediately.

Gobhi 65

SERVES 4
sunflower oil, for
  deep-frying
1 cauliflower, cut into
  roughly 2.5 cm
  (1 inch) florets

FOR THE BATTER
1 cm (½ inch) piece
  of fresh root ginger,
  peeled and grated
2 tablespoons shop-
  bought chilli-garlic
  sauce
120 g (4¼ oz)
  cornflour
120 g (4¼ oz) rice flour
½ teaspoon salt
230 ml (8 fl oz) water

FOR THE STIR-FRY
2 tablespoons
  sunflower oil
2.5 cm (1 inch) piece
  of fresh root ginger,
  peeled and julienned
8–10 fresh curry leaves
2 tablespoons shop-
  bought chilli-garlic
  sauce
2 tablespoons water

This is my veggie take on the world-famous Indian-restaurant dish known as Chicken 65, the origin of which is hotly debated. Some say it was first served at a restaurant in Chennai where it was number 65 on the menu, while others say it is named after the 65 spices used to make it. Either way, it's delicious! Although my cauliflower version doesn't use 65 spices, I feel it captures something of the flavour of the popular chicken dish.

1 Put all the batter ingredients in a bowl and mix well with a spoon.

2 Heat enough oil for deep-frying in a deep, heavy-based saucepan or deep-fat fryer to 170°C (340°F). (Maintain this throughout cooking.) Dip each cauliflower floret in the batter, then slide it carefully into the hot oil. Cook over a medium heat for a couple of minutes on each side until golden and crispy. Remove the cooked florets with a slotted spoon and transfer to a plate lined with kitchen paper to drain.

3 To make the stir-fry, heat the oil in a separate pan or a wok over a high heat. Add the ginger and curry leaves to the pan and let them sizzle for a minute, then add the chilli-garlic sauce, followed by the measured water. Allow the water to come to the boil, then add the fried cauliflower, stir quickly to cover the florets with the mixture in the pan, then remove from the pan and serve immediately.

Baigan Bhaja

SERVES 4
1 aubergine
½ teaspoon salt
½ teaspoon chilli
  powder
sunflower oil, for
  deep-frying
sea salt flakes
coriander and spinach
  chutney and/or
  tomato chutney,
  to serve

FOR THE BATTER
150 g (5½ oz) gram
  flour (besan)
¾ teaspoon salt
½ teaspoon chilli
  powder
½ teaspoon turmeric
about 300 ml (½ pint)
  water

These pakoras are flavoured with nothing other than salt, turmeric and chilli, yet the flavour is outstanding, no doubt due to the beautifully tender aubergine encased in a crisp, tasty coating. Pair them with coriander and spinach chutney or tomato chutney.

1 Cut the aubergine vertically into thin slices with a thickness of no more than 5 mm (¼ inch). Rub the flesh with the salt and chilli powder then leave to stand for 10 minutes. (This helps to release excess moisture in the aubergine flesh.)

2 To make the batter, combine the gram flour, salt and spices in a bowl, then gradually add just enough of the measured water to form a smooth batter with a thin coating consistency.

3 Heat enough oil for deep-frying in a deep-fat fryer or large, heavy-based saucepan to 190°C (375°F). Line a sheet with some kitchen paper. Working with one slice of aubergine at a time, press it between 2 sheets of kitchen paper to extract excess moisture, then dip the slice in the batter, add it to the hot oil and fry for 1 minute on each side, until deep golden brown and crispy. Transfer to the paper-lined plate and leave to drain excess oil while you fry the remaining aubergine slices. Season with sea salt flakes and serve hot with your preferred chutney.

Dal Papdi Chaat

SERVES 4

FOR THE PAPDI

300 g (10½ oz) plain
  flour, plus extra for
  dusting
½ teaspoon salt
½ teaspoon chilli
  powder
½ teaspoon ground
  cumin
3 tablespoons
  sunflower oil, plus
  extra for deep-frying
120 ml (4 fl oz) water

FOR THE DAL

250 g (9 oz) chana dal
  (split chickpeas)
1 litre (1¾ pints)
  boiling water
1 teaspoon salt
½ teaspoon ground
  turmeric
2 tablespoons ghee
1 green chilli, finely
  chopped
1 teaspoon ground
  cumin
1 teaspoon chaat
  masala

This is one of those dishes that I could happily live off for the rest of my life. The crispness of the papdi with the moreish masala dal and the magical chutneys is the most dreamy combination of all! You can prepare the papdi, dal and chutneys in advance, but put the dish together only when you are ready to eat to retain the satisfying crispiness of the papdi.

1 Start by preparing the papdi. Put the flour, salt, chilli powder, cumin and oil into a bowl and mix well. Slowly add the measured water as you mix with your hand to form a soft dough. Knead the dough for 2 minutes. Cover the bowl with a clean tea towel and leave to rest for 15 minutes.

2 Heat enough oil for deep-frying in a deep, heavy-based saucepan or deep-fat fryer to 170°C (340°F). (Maintain this temperature throughout cooking.)

3 Meanwhile, divide the dough into 4 equal portions and roll out each portion on a lightly floured surface into a thin sheet (in any shape you like) to a depth of roughly 2 mm (⅛ inch). Now cut these sheets into thin strips, diamond shapes or squares. Place the shapes carefully into the hot oil and fry over a medium–low heat for 3–4 minutes until golden and crispy. Remove the papdi from the hot oil using a slotted spoon, transfer to a plate lined with kitchen paper and leave to cool while you prepare the dal.

4 Put the chana dal into a pan with the measured boiling water, salt and turmeric and cook over a medium–low heat for 1 hour until the dal is soft. If it becomes too thick during cooking, stir in another 100 ml (3½ fl oz) boiling water.

100 ml (3 ½ fl oz)
  natural yogurt
50 ml (2 fl oz) water
tamarind jaggery
  chutney, to taste
coriander yogurt
  chutney, to taste
pinch of salt
pinch of chilli powder
1 red onion, finely
  chopped
1 green chilli, finely
  chopped

5   Heat the ghee in a small saucepan, then add the chilli. Once the ghee begins to sizzle, take the pan off the heat, add the cumin and chaat masala and mix well. Pour this mixture over the cooked dal and mix well. Leave to cool slightly.

6   When you're ready to serve, put the yogurt into a bowl and stir in the measured water to thin it out.

7   Place the cooled papdis on a plate, top with the warm dal, then drizzle over the yogurt and chutneys. Sprinkle with the salt and chilli powder, then the onion and green chilli. Serve immediately.

Fish Chop

SERVES 4
3 large eggs
300 g (10 ½ oz)
  skinless cod fillets
1 onion, finely
  chopped
handful of fresh
  coriander leaves,
  finely chopped
2 garlic cloves, finely
  chopped
2 small green chillies,
  finely chopped
½ teaspoon salt
sunflower oil, for
  deep-frying
sea salt flakes
sichuan sauce or
  coriander and
  spinach chutney,
  to serve

FOR THE COATING
2 eggs, lightly beaten
100 g (3 ½ oz) golden
  breadcrumbs

These delicious fish chops from the streets of Kolkata can be enjoyed hot or cold with a variety of chutneys. If you want something fiery, try them with a sichuan chilli sauce; if you'd prefer something mild, opt for a coriander and spinach chutney.

1 Put the eggs into a small saucepan, cover with water and boil for 10 minutes. Drain and leave to cool, then shell the eggs and mash them in a bowl.

2 In a food processor, blitz the cod to a coarse paste. Add the fish to the mashed eggs, along with the onion, coriander, garlic, chillies and salt. Mix thoroughly so that the flavours are well combined.

3 Shape the mixture into balls the size of a lemon, then press to flatten them slightly. Dip each one in the beaten egg, then roll them in the breadcrumbs until fully coated.

4 Heat enough oil for deep-frying in a deep-fat fryer or a deep, heavy-based saucepan to 170–180°C (340–350°F). Line a plate with some kitchen paper. Fry the chops a few at a time for about 2 minutes, until they are cooked through and golden. Transfer to the paper-lined plate and leave to drain excess oil while you fry the remaining chops.

5 Season with sea salt flakes and serve warm with your choice of sauce or chutney.

Masala Papdi

MAKES 1 PLATEFUL
100 g (3½ oz) plain
   flour, plus extra for
   dusting
1 tablespoon kasuri
   methi (dried
   fenugreek leaves)
¼ teaspoon salt
¼ teaspoon carom
   seeds (ajwain)
¼ teaspoon garam
   masala
¼ teaspoon chilli
   powder
¼ teaspoon ground
   turmeric
1 tablespoon sunflower
   oil, plus extra for
   deep-frying
about 45 ml
   (3 tablespoons) water

This is the most popular snack in my house. It used to be my favourite snack growing up and now it's my kids' favourite, too. My mum would always keep a box of papdi in the cupboard and refill it as soon as it was empty. I make them often but not as often as she did, as I find they disappear faster than I can make them. No one can ever have just one.

1 Mix all the dry ingredients together in a bowl. Add the 1 tablespoon of oil and rub in with your fingertips until the mixture resembles breadcrumbs. Then gradually add just enough of the water, or a little more if needed, to bring the mixture together into a soft dough. Cover and let it rest for 5 minutes.

2 Divide the dough into 4 portions. Roll out each portion on a lightly floured work surface into a thin sheet about 15–18 cm (6–7 inches) square. Using a sharp knife, cut the sheet into strips about 2.5 cm (1 inch) wide.

3 Heat enough oil for deep-frying in a deep-fat fryer or deep, heavy-based pan (ensuring the pan is no more than one-third full) to about 170°C (340°F). Line a plate with kitchen paper.

4 Deep-fry the pastry strips, in batches, for a few seconds, then turn over and cook until golden. Transfer to the paper-lined plate to absorb the excess oil and cool while you fry the remaining pastry strips. They will crisp up as they cool down.

5 The masala papdi will keep in an airtight container for up to 2 weeks.

Masala Peanuts

MAKES 1 LARGE
BOWLFUL

60 g (2¼ oz) gram
flour (besan)
30 g (1 oz) rice flour
20 g (¾ oz) cornflour
1 teaspoon chilli
powder
½ teaspoon ground
turmeric
½ teaspoon garlic salt
250 g (9 oz) roasted,
unsalted peanuts
2 teaspoons sunflower
oil, plus extra for
shallow-frying
60 ml (4 tablespoons)
water

These crispy, spicy and delicious peanuts are a very popular snack in India, where you will find them in all corner shops and sweet shops. They are so easy to make at home, and perfect with a cup of tea or a drink. The only problem is that once you start eating them, it's quite difficult to stop!

1 Mix all the flours and spices together in a bowl, then stir in the peanuts.

2 Add the 2 teaspoons of oil and mix well, then gradually whisk in the water to make a thick gloopy batter that coats the peanuts.

3 Heat enough oil for shallow-frying in a frying pan. Line a plate with kitchen paper.

4 Working in a couple of batches, carefully add the coated peanuts to the hot oil, separating them as you go if you can, and cook over a medium heat for 2–3 minutes until golden and crispy. Transfer to the paper-lined plate to absorb the excess oil and cool while you fry the remaining peanuts. They will crisp up more once they have cooled down.

5 The peanuts will keep in an airtight container for up to 2 weeks.

VEGETABLES

Lentil and Mango Salad

FOR THE SALAD

100 g (3½ oz) moong
dal (split mung beans)
1 red onion, finely
chopped
1 cucumber, diced
1 carrot, grated
1 raw green or unripe
mango, peeled and
finely chopped

FOR THE TADKA

1 tablespoon rapeseed
oil
1 teaspoon black
mustard seeds
1 teaspoon chilli flakes
½ teaspoon salt
1 tablespoon lemon
juice

You might wonder what lentils are doing in a salad with mangoes, but let me tell you that I was just as surprised when I tried this at my friend Jayashree's house. She often makes it in the summer, when mangoes are in season, and it's quickly become one of my favourites too. Don't worry if you can't find Indian green mangoes – you can use ordinary hard, unripe mangoes from the supermarket instead.

1 Soak the moong dal in a bowl of cold water for 3–4 hours, then drain thoroughly. Return to the bowl with the rest of the salad ingredients.

2 To make the tadka, heat the oil in a small pan and add the mustard seeds. Once they start to sizzle, remove the pan from the heat and add the chilli flakes and salt. Pour this over the salad.

3 Drizzle the salad with the lemon juice, toss it all well and then serve.

4 This will last in the refrigerator for a couple of days.

Beetroot, Carrot and Peanut Salad

SERVES 4

FOR THE SALAD
50 g (1¾ oz) roasted
  peanuts
4 uncooked beetroot,
  about 400 g (14 oz),
  grated
1 red onion, finely
  chopped
20 g (¾ oz) fresh
  coriander, finely
  chopped
1 carrot, grated
2 tablespoons lime
  juice
½ teaspoon salt

FOR THE TADKA
1 tablespoon
  groundnut oil
1 teaspoon cumin
  seeds
2 green chillies, finely
  chopped

I was blown away by this salad when my friend Pranoti made it for me – I never would have thought of combining peanuts and beetroot. Even my kids, who don't like beetroot that much, absolutely love this quick dish. It gets so much flavour and crunch from the peanuts and cumin seeds, I think it's a must-have on summer tables.

1 Use a pestle and mortar to coarsely crush the peanuts, then put them into a large bowl with the rest of the salad ingredients.

2 To make the tadka, heat the oil in a small pan and add the cumin seeds. Once they start to sizzle, add the green chillies, give them a stir, then take the pan off the heat. Pour the tadka over the salad, toss well and serve.

3 This will keep in the refrigerator for a couple of days.

Courgette Bharta

FOR THE
COURGETTES

4 courgettes, about
  800 g (1 lb 12 oz)
1 teaspoon rapeseed oil
¼ teaspoon salt
¼ teaspoon freshly
  ground black pepper

FOR THE BHARTA

1 teaspoon rapeseed oil
1 teaspoon black
  mustard seeds
1 cm (½ inch)
  fresh root ginger,
  peeled and cut into
  matchsticks
¼ teaspoon salt
½ teaspoon chilli
  powder
1 tablespoon lime juice

Usually in India the word 'bharta' describes a roasted aubergine dish, but here I'm making it with courgettes. I was inspired by my friend Abha, who made bharta with potatoes when I visited her home. I wanted to try her recipe with courgettes and found they work beautifully with these simple spices. You can serve this warm, or cold as a salad.

1 Preheat the oven to 200°C (400°F), Gas Mark 6. Slice the courgettes into 5 mm (¼ inch) discs. Put them into a bowl with the oil, salt and pepper and mix well. Spread the slices on a baking tray, making sure they do not overlap, and roast for 10 minutes.

2 To make the bharta, heat the oil in a pan and add the mustard seeds. Once they start to sizzle, add the ginger and let it cook for 1 minute. Add the salt, chilli powder and roast courgette slices and mix well.

3 Squeeze the lime juice over the top, give it a stir and serve. This is best enjoyed immediately but can also be served warm or cold as a salad.

Potato, Paneer and Chickpea Curry

SERVES 4
2 tablespoons
  sunflower oil
2 onions, roughly
  chopped
4 tomatoes, roughly
  chopped
1 small green chilli,
  chopped
2 garlic cloves,
  chopped
2.5 cm (1 inch) piece
  of fresh root ginger,
  peeled and chopped
200 ml (7 fl oz) water
1 cinnamon stick
1½ teaspoons salt
1 teaspoon granulated
  sugar
2 teaspoons garam
  masala
½ teaspoon ground
  turmeric
½ teaspoon chilli
  powder
100 g (3½ oz) paneer,
  cubed
2 floury potatoes,
  boiled, peeled and
  cubed
400 g (14 oz) can
  chickpeas
soft kachori, rice or
  chapattis, to serve

Soft, fluffy potato and cubes of paneer soak up the flavours of the sauce in this light, delicious curry, while the chickpeas add a lovely texture. This dish is very popular in Kolkata and best teamed with soft kachori, but if you want a healthier version, serve it with rice or chapattis.

1 Heat 1 tablespoon of the oil in a saucepan over a medium heat. Add the onions, tomatoes, chilli, garlic and ginger and cook for 10 minutes, or until everything is softened.

2 Transfer the mixture to a blender or food processor, add 100 ml (3½ fl oz) of the measured water and blend to a smooth paste.

3 Heat the remaining oil in a saucepan over a medium heat. Add the cinnamon stick and cook for a few seconds, then stir in the onion and tomato paste. Cover the pan with a lid and cook over a low heat for 10–15 minutes, until well cooked.

4 Add the salt, sugar, spices and the remaining 100 ml (3½ fl oz) measured water to the pan and mix well. Stir in the paneer, potatoes and the chickpeas along with their canning liquid. Cover and cook for about 10 minutes, until the sauce thickens and the potatoes are tender. Serve the curry hot with soft kachori, rice or chapattis.

Tamarind Aubergine Curry

SERVES 2

FOR THE CURRY
1 tablespoon sunflower
  oil
pinch of asafoetida
2 onions, thinly sliced
1 tablespoon fennel
  seeds
1 teaspoon chilli
  powder
1 teaspoon ground
  ginger
200 ml (7 fl oz) water
1 teaspoon sugar
1 teaspoon tamarind
  paste

FOR THE
AUBERGINE

1 aubergine, cut into
  fingers 5–7.5 cm
  (2–3 inches) long
¼ teaspoon salt
2–3 tablespoons
  sunflower oil

If you are an aubergine fan, then this dish is sure to become your next favourite thing. The fried aubergine picks up on the aniseed notes of the fennel and the sour kick from the tamarind, and the whole combination is just heavenly. Be careful not to taste it too much along the way, as you might have nothing left to eat at the end! Serve with some rice or paratha.

1 To prepare the aubergine, place it on a plate, sprinkle with the salt and set aside for 10 minutes.

2 Meanwhile, heat the oil for the curry in a pan, add the asafoetida and let it sizzle for a few seconds. Then add the onions and cook over a medium heat for 10 minutes until golden.

3 Heat the oil for the aubergine in a large frying pan. Pat the aubergine fingers dry, add them to the hot oil and cook over a high heat for 2 minutes until golden.

4 While the aubergine is cooking, heat a small frying pan, add the fennel seeds and dry-roast over a low heat for a minute. Then use a pestle and mortar to crush them.

5 Add the crushed fennel seeds to the onions and cook for a minute. Then stir in the ground spices and add the fried aubergine with the measured water. Cook over a low heat for 10 minutes.

6 Stir in the sugar and tamarind and cook over a high heat for 5 minutes until the sauce thickens, then serve.

Mixed Vegetable Curry

SERVES 4

2 tablespoons
  sunflower oil
1 teaspoon cumin
  seeds
1 teaspoon black
  mustard seeds
1 bay leaf
2 onions, finely
  chopped
1 green chilli, finely
  chopped
2 garlic cloves, grated
2.5 cm (1 inch) piece
  of fresh root ginger,
  peeled and grated
1 teaspoon salt
1 teaspoon ground
  turmeric
1 teaspoon chilli
  powder
1 teaspoon garam
  masala
1 teaspoon amchur
  (mango powder)
½ teaspoon sugar
2 tomatoes, finely
  chopped
100 ml (3½ fl oz)
  boiling water

We all have those oddments of veg in the refrigerator – a lonely carrot, some peas, the last bit of a cauliflower or half an onion. This recipe is the perfect way to use up all those vegetable leftovers. I have used three different veg here, but you can add a few other ingredients if you have them and make this curry your own. Serve it with some rice or chapattis and a nice raita for a lovely meal.

1 Heat the oil in a pan and add the cumin and mustard seeds and the bay leaf. Once they start to sizzle, add the chopped onions with the green chilli and cook over a medium heat for 10 minutes until golden. Then add the garlic and ginger and cook for a minute.

2 Meanwhile, heat the oil for the vegetables in a large frying pan. Add all of the vegetables and cook them over a medium–high heat for 8–10 minutes until lightly coloured.

**FOR THE
VEGETABLES**

2 tablespoons
  sunflower oil
½ cauliflower, cut into
  small florets
2 carrots, cut into
  small pieces
200 g (7 oz) fine green
  beans, cut into 2.5 cm
  (1 inch) pieces

3 Stir the salt, ground spices and sugar into the onions
   with the tomatoes and cook for a minute. Then add the
   vegetables and pour in the measured boiling water. Cover
   and cook over a low–medium heat for 10 minutes until
   the cauliflower is soft, then serve.

Garlicky Mushroom Sabji

SERVES 4

2 tablespoons
  sunflower oil
1 teaspoon fenugreek
  seeds
1 onion, thinly sliced
4 garlic cloves, thinly
  sliced
600 g (1 lb 5 oz)
  chestnut mushrooms,
  thinly sliced
100 ml (3 ½ fl oz)
  natural yogurt
½ teaspoon salt
1 teaspoon ground
  coriander
1 teaspoon ground
  cumin
1 teaspoon chilli
  powder
handful of chives,
  finely chopped

I have made many different mushroom curries over the years, but I wanted to try a new approach. So I devised this mushroom sabji with tons of flavour but without a sauce so that you can scoop it up with some naan or chapattis. Using just a handful of spices and some yogurt, you really can't go wrong with this simple dish. Serve with naan or a dal such as the Spinach and Coconut Dal.

1 Heat the oil in a pan, add the fenugreek seeds and cook over a medium–low heat for a few seconds until they start to change colour. Add the onion and cook over a medium heat for 8–10 minutes until golden. Then add the garlic and cook for a minute.

2 Add the mushrooms and cook over a high heat for 5 minutes, then turn the heat down to low.

3 Mix the yogurt, salt and ground spices together in a bowl, then add to the mushrooms and cook for a minute, stirring constantly to prevent the yogurt from splitting.

4 Cook over a medium heat for 10 minutes until the liquid has almost all cooked off.

5 Add the chives and serve.

Paneer and Purple Sprouting Broccoli Sabji

SERVES 4

1 tablespoon sunflower oil

1 teaspoon mustard seeds

10 curry leaves

2 red onions, finely chopped

225 g (8 oz) paneer, cut into 1 cm (½ inch) dice

225 g (8 oz) purple sprouting broccoli, cut into small chunks

½ teaspoon salt

½ teaspoon ground turmeric

½ teaspoon chilli powder

½ teaspoon amchur (mango powder)

50 ml (2 fl oz) boiling water

If you're thinking that this sounds like an unusual combination then, yes, you are definitely right. But it is one that works a treat. The earthiness of the broccoli goes well with soft, spice-infused paneer. This dish is great served with chapatti, or in a wrap with some spicy chutney, or as a side dish with lentils and rice.

1   Heat the oil in a saucepan over a low heat. Add the mustard seeds and let them sizzle for a few seconds, then mix in the curry leaves and onions and cook over a low heat for 5 minutes, until the onions have softened.

2   Meanwhile, soak the paneer cubes in a bowl of hot water for a minimum of 5 minutes.

3   Stir the broccoli, salt, turmeric, chilli powder, amchur and the measured boiling water (which will create a little steam) into the saucepan. Cover the pan with a lid and cook over a low heat for 5–6 minutes or until the broccoli has softened slightly.

4   Drain the paneer and add it to the saucepan, mixing well. Increase the heat to high and cook for 1 minute, then serve immediately.

New Potato and Tomato Curry

SERVES 4

FOR THE
POTATOES

2–4 tablespoons
rapeseed oil
600 g (1 lb 5 oz) new
potatoes, cut in half

FOR THE CURRY

1 tablespoon rapeseed
oil
pinch of asafoetida
1 teaspoon black
mustard seeds
10 fresh curry leaves
1 green chilli, finely
chopped
1 tablespoon sesame
seeds
2.5 cm (1 inch) piece
of fresh root ginger,
peeled and grated
4 tomatoes, finely
chopped
1 teaspoon salt
1 teaspoon ground
turmeric
1 teaspoon garam
masala
1 teaspoon sugar
200 ml (7 fl oz) boiling
water
juice of ½ lime
20 g (¾ oz) fresh
coriander leaves,
finely chopped

One for the whole family, even the fussy eaters can't say no
to this simple curry. The slightly fried potatoes absorb all
the amazing heat and sourness from the spices and tomatoes
and become juicy and delicious. Use new potatoes in season
when available, but otherwise ordinary potatoes cut into
small pieces. Enjoy it with fried flatbread, but it's good with
rice, too.

1 Heat the oil for the potatoes in a large frying pan. Add the
potatoes, cut-side down, in a single layer and cook over
a medium–high heat for 1–2 minutes until beautifully
golden. You may have to do this in batches, depending
on the size of your pan.

2 Meanwhile, start making the curry. Heat the oil in a pan
and add the asafoetida. Once it starts to sizzle, add the
mustard seeds with the curry leaves and chilli and cook
over a low heat until they start to pop. Then add the
sesame seeds and ginger and cook for a few seconds.

3 Add the tomatoes and cook over a medium heat for
5 minutes until they start to soften. Stir in the salt, ground
spices and sugar and cook for a minute.

4 Add the golden potatoes and the measured boiling water,
cover and cook over a low to medium heat for about
10 minutes until the potatoes are cooked through.

5 Add the lime juice and coriander, mix well, then serve.

Tandoori Paneer Curry

SERVES 4

450 g (1 lb) paneer, cut into 2.5 cm (1 inch) cubes

6 tablespoons sunflower oil

2 onions, finely chopped

2.5 cm (1 inch) piece of fresh root ginger, peeled and finely chopped

4 garlic cloves, finely chopped

1 green chilli, finely chopped

400 g (14 oz) can chopped tomatoes

100 ml (3½ fl oz) water

½ teaspoon salt

½ teaspoon ground turmeric

1 teaspoon chilli powder

1 teaspoon garam masala

1 teaspoon tandoori masala

3 tablespoons double cream

By cooking paneer in tandoori masala with some yogurt and spices, you give it a delicious coating. When you then add the paneer to a tasty curry, you layer flavour upon flavour to make the ultimate dish for paneer-lovers. I have two of those at home – both my kids are big fans of paneer and they love this dish.

1 Put all the marinade ingredients into a large bowl and mix well. Now add the paneer cubes and combine gently to ensure all are coated well. Cover the bowl and leave to marinate for 30 minutes.

2 Heat 4 tablespoons of the oil in a saucepan over a medium–low heat. Add the paneer cubes without crowding them to ensure they cook evenly. Cook for 1 minute, then turn them over and cook for 1 minute more until golden. Leave the paneer to one side.

3 Heat the remaining oil in the same pan and add the onions. Cook these over a medium–low heat for 8–10 minutes until nicely golden.

FOR THE MARINADE

150 ml (¼ pint) natural yogurt

¼ teaspoon salt

½ teaspoon chilli powder

¼ teaspoon ground turmeric

1 teaspoon tandoori masala

4 Stir the ginger, garlic and green chilli into the onions in the pan and cook for 1 minute. Now mix in the canned tomatoes and measured water, cover the pan with a lid and cook over a low heat for 15 minutes.

5 Add the salt and spices to the pan, followed by the cooked paneer cubes. Combine well, then stir in the cream and serve immediately.

Ultimate Potato Sabji

SERVES 4
50 ml (2 fl oz) rapeseed
  oil
pinch of asafoetida
1 teaspoon cumin
  seeds
1 onion, finely
  chopped
2.5 cm (1 inch) piece
  of fresh root ginger,
  peeled and finely
  chopped
4 garlic cloves, finely
  chopped
1 green chilli, finely
  chopped
4 medium potatoes,
  peeled and cut into
  2.5 cm (1 inch) dice
½ teaspoon salt
½ teaspoon ground
  turmeric
½ teaspoon chaat
  masala
1 teaspoon chilli
  powder
1 teaspoon garam
  masala
1 teaspoon amchur
  (mango powder)
handful of fresh
  coriander leaves,
  finely chopped

At first I was having trouble finding the right name for this sabji (vegetable dish). It is spicy, moreishly sour and the most delicious, quick and flavourful potato dish you will ever make. Then the word 'ultimate' came to mind, because that's what it is – simply the best potato sabji!

1 Heat the oil in a saucepan over a medium–low heat. Add the asafoetida and cumin and let the mixture sizzle for a few seconds, then stir in the onion and cook for 4–5 minutes until softened.

2 Add the ginger, garlic and chilli to the pan, mix well and continue to cook over a medium–low heat for 1 minute. Next, stir in the potatoes and cook over a high heat for 1 minute. Now cover the pan with a lid and cook over a low heat for 10–12 minutes until the potatoes are cooked through and soft.

3 Add the salt and spices to the pan with the coriander, mix well and cook over a high heat for 1 minute more, then serve immediately.

Cauliflower Masala

2 tablespoons
 sunflower oil
1 teaspoon fennel
 seeds
1 teaspoon cumin
 seeds
3 onions, thinly sliced
2.5 cm (1 inch) piece
 of fresh root ginger,
 peeled and finely
 chopped
4 garlic cloves, finely
 chopped
1 green chilli, finely
 chopped
2 tomatoes, thinly
 sliced
1 teaspoon salt
1 teaspoon ground
 turmeric
2 teaspoons ground
 coriander
1 teaspoon garam
 masala
1 teaspoon chilli
 powder
1 tablespoon shop-
 bought chilli-garlic
 sauce
1 cauliflower, cut into
 florets
8–10 mint leaves,
 finely chopped

This is a stunning veggie dish, yet it's easy to make and ready in a flash! Cauliflower is one of my favourite vegetables. It can be cooked in so many ways and lends itself to all sorts of spicing. For this recipe I add all the flavours from my spice box as well as some chilli-garlic sauce for extra depth. You can use any shop-bought chilli-garlic sauce, but if you don't have any, substitute harissa or a chilli-tomato sauce – either works beautifully.

1 Heat the sunflower oil in a saucepan over a medium–low heat. Add the fennel and cumin seeds and cook for 1–2 minutes until they begin to sizzle. Stir in the onions and cook over a medium–low heat for 8–10 minutes until golden.

2 Add the ginger, garlic and chilli to the saucepan, stir well and cook for 1 minute. Add the tomatoes and mix well. Stir the salt and spices in, then add the chilli-garlic sauce.

3 Finally, add the cauliflower to the saucepan and mix well, then cover the pan with a lid and cook over a medium–low heat for 10–12 minutes until the florets are softened and cooked through. Take the pan off the heat, sprinkle over the mint and serve immediately.

Sour and Spicy Okra with Potatoes

SERVES 4

1 tablespoon sunflower
  oil
1 teaspoon cumin
  seeds
3 garlic cloves, finely
  chopped
2 onions, thinly sliced
1 potato, unpeeled,
  thinly sliced
1 teaspoon salt
1 teaspoon garam
  masala
1 teaspoon chilli
  powder
1 teaspoon chaat
  masala
1 tomato, thinly sliced
300 g (10½ oz)
  okra, quartered
  lengthways
1 teaspoon lemon juice

This is something my mum makes all the time to accompany dal and chapatti. I do like it that way, but I love to put the leftovers into a wrap or toastie and serve it with tomato chutney – a brilliant combination.

1 Heat the oil in a pan over a medium-to-low heat and add the cumin seeds. Once they begin to sizzle, add the garlic and cook for a minute, until it is just beginning to colour. Add the onions and cook for 2 minutes so that they begin to soften. Now turn the heat to high, add the potato and cook for 2 minutes.

2 Add the salt, garam masala, chilli powder and chaat masala, plus the tomato and okra. Cover and cook for 10 minutes over a low heat, until the vegetables are tender.

3 Remove the lid and finish over a high heat for 2 minutes, to crisp the vegetables slightly. Stir in the lemon juice and serve.

4 This will keep in an airtight container in the refrigerator for 4–5 days. Reheat thoroughly before serving.

Tandoori Veg Kebab

MAKES 8

FOR THE BULGUR WHEAT

150 g (5½ oz) bulgur wheat

900 ml (1½ pints) boiling water

1 tablespoon lemon juice

1 tablespoon rapeseed oil

¼ teaspoon salt

¼ teaspoon freshly ground black pepper

FOR THE SKEWERS

1 sweet potato, halved lengthways and cut into 1 cm (½ inch) slices

1 courgette, cut into 5 mm (¼ inch) circles

1 red onion, cut into thin wedges

100 g (3½ oz) natural yogurt

1 tablespoon tandoori masala

¼ teaspoon chilli powder

¼ teaspoon salt

oil, for brushing

You don't really need a barbecue to enjoy these vegetable kebabs. They can also be cooked under a grill or in a frying pan – whatever you have handy. The combination of courgettes, sweet potatoes, red onions and tandoori masala is so simple yet so amazing. I've made this a substantial main course by serving the kebabs with bulgur wheat. You'll find the yogurt dressing adds a lovely finish and flavour.

1 Put the bulgur wheat into a heatproof bowl and cover with the measured boiling water. Leave to soak for 20 minutes, then drain well. (If you are using bamboo skewers, soak them in water now too. You'll need 8 of them.)

2 Wipe out the bowl and return the bulgur to it. Add the lemon juice, oil, salt and pepper, and mix well. Set aside.

3 To prepare the kebabs, par-cook the sliced sweet potato in a pan of boiling water for 2 minutes only. Rinse and drain.

4 Put the courgette and onion into a large bowl and add the sweet potato slices. In a small bowl, mix the yogurt, tandoori masala, chilli powder and salt together and pour this all over the veg. Stir to make sure the veg are well covered with the marinade.

FOR THE DRESSING
100 g (3½ oz) natural
   yogurt
¼ teaspoon ground
   cumin
a pinch of salt

5 Preheat your barbecue or grill. Take the skewers and
thread the veg on to them as you like. Brush a little oil
over the top. When the barbecue or grill is hot, cook for
20 minutes, turning occasionally, until golden.

6 In a small bowl, mix the dressing ingredients. Spread
the bulgur wheat on a serving platter, lay the skewers on
top and drizzle over the dressing to serve. These are best
eaten immediately.

MEAT & FISH

Yogurt Chicken Curry

SERVES 4

200 ml (7 fl oz) natural
  yogurt
1 teaspoon salt
1 teaspoon garam
  masala
½ teaspoon ground
  turmeric
½ teaspoon chilli
  powder
2 garlic cloves, grated
600 g (1 lb 5 oz)
  boneless, skinless
  chicken thighs, cut
  into 3 cm (1¼ inch)
  pieces
2 tablespoons
  sunflower oil
1 teaspoon cumin
  seeds
2 tomatoes, thinly
  sliced
20 g (¾ oz) fresh
  coriander leaves,
  finely chopped

I have shared other yogurt chicken recipes in my previous books, but this is the easiest version and one of the most delicious ways to cook chicken – and it's my kids' favourite. I have to admit that I usually make this with chicken on the bone, as the bones add flavour to the curry. But it does take a bit more time to cook and I know many people prefer boneless chicken. This is a foolproof curry that works every single time, and you can enjoy it with any flatbreads or rice.

1 Mix the yogurt, salt, spices and garlic together in a bowl. Add the chicken pieces and turn until well coated in the marinade. Let the chicken marinate while you prepare the curry base.

2 Heat the oil in a pan and add the cumin seeds. Once they start to sizzle, add the tomatoes and cook over a medium heat for 5 minutes until they start to soften.

3 Add the marinated chicken with any excess marinade and mix well, then bring to the boil. Cover and cook over a medium–low heat for 15 minutes or until the chicken is cooked through.

4 Sprinkle with the coriander and serve.

Masala Chicken

SERVES 4

50 g (1¾ oz) gram
flour (besan)
70 ml (2½ fl oz)
natural yogurt
½ teaspoon kala
namak (black salt)
1 teaspoon Kashmiri
chilli powder
1 teaspoon kasuri
methi (dried
fenugreek leaves)
½ teaspoon garam
masala
½ teaspoon ground
cumin
4 boneless, skinless
chicken thighs, cut
into 5 cm (2 inches)
pieces
3 tablespoons
sunflower oil

When I created this dish, I had no idea how it would turn out.
But once I had tasted it, I couldn't stop eating it and since
then I have been making it a lot when entertaining or cooking
for friends. You can also cook it on a hot barbecue or in a
hot oven for about 10 minutes until cooked through. This is
flavourful enough to serve on its own, although it's great with
a ginger and chilli chutney. Just make sure to cook extra; it's
devilishly moreish.

1 Heat a frying pan, add the flour and toast over a low heat
   for about 2 minutes or until it starts to change colour,
   stirring constantly.

2 Put the toasted flour into a bowl with the yogurt, salt and
   spices and mix together well. Add the chicken pieces and
   turn in the marinade until well coated.

3 Heat the oil in a pan. Carefully add the marinated chicken
   pieces to the hot oil and cook over a medium–low heat for
   8–10 minutes, turning halfway through, until golden and
   cooked through.

Korma-Style Chicken Curry

SERVES 4

2 tablespoons
  sunflower oil
1 cinnamon stick,
  broken up into small
  pieces
2 onions, roughly
  chopped
1 green chilli, roughly
  chopped
2 garlic cloves, roughly
  chopped
2.5 cm (1 inch) piece
  of fresh root ginger,
  peeled and roughly
  chopped
50 g (1¾ oz) cashew
  nuts
1 tablespoon white
  poppy seeds
100 ml (3½ fl oz) water
1 teaspoon salt
1 teaspoon garam
  masala
1 teaspoon chilli powder
200 ml (7 fl oz) boiling
  water
650 g (1 lb 7 oz)
  boneless, skinless
  chicken thighs, cut
  into 5 cm (2 inches)
  pieces
1 tablespoon double
  cream
20 g (¾ oz) fresh
  coriander leaves,
  finely chopped

When you have a chicken korma in a restaurant, it tends to be sweet, sometimes with raisins and quite pale. I am not a big fan of that style of korma and once you have tried my version you may well prefer mine, too. The simple spices used in the sauce lend the chicken a lovely warmth, while you get a beautiful creaminess from the cashews, poppy seeds and onions, resulting in a deliciously delicate curry. Serve with spiced layered flatbread, chapattis or naan, or with rice.

1 Heat the oil in a pan and add the cinnamon. Once it starts to sizzle, add the onions with the green chilli and cook over a medium heat for 5 minutes until they start to colour.

2 Add the garlic, ginger and cashew nuts and cook over a medium heat for 5 minutes until lightly golden. Stir in the poppy seeds and then pour in the measured water.

3 Transfer the mixture to a blender and blitz until smooth, then return to the pan.

4 Stir in the salt, ground spices and measured boiling water, then add the chicken pieces. Cover and cook over a medium heat for 10 minutes until the chicken is cooked through.

5 Add the cream and coriander, then serve.

Whole Tandoori-Style Chicken

SERVES 3–4

1 whole chicken,
  around 1.5 kg
  (3 lb 5 oz)

FOR THE FIRST
MARINADE

1 teaspoon salt
1 teaspoon Kashmiri
  chilli powder
10 garlic cloves, finely
  chopped
3–4 cm (1¼–1½
  inches) piece of fresh
  root ginger, peeled
  and finely chopped
4 tablespoons lemon
  juice

FOR THE SECOND
MARINADE

200 ml (7 fl oz)
  natural yogurt
1 tablespoon ground
  coriander
1 tablespoon garam
  masala
2 tablespoons tandoori
  masala powder
1 teaspoon amchur
  (mango powder)
1 teaspoon salt
1 tablespoon mustard
  oil
40 g (1½ oz) fresh
  coriander, leaves and
  stems finely chopped

I have tried and tested this famous dish with various spices over the years and have found this version works perfectly every time. It's cooked in a regular oven rather than a tandoor, but it also works well on the barbecue, which lends the dish an extra smoky flavour. If you prefer, use small cuts of chicken, such as drumsticks or thighs, instead of the whole bird. This dish is great served with salad or pulao.

1   Combine the ingredients for the first marinade in a small bowl and mix well. Rub this all over the chicken, then cover and leave to rest in the refrigerator for 1 hour.

2   Put all the ingredients for the second marinade, except the fresh coriander, into another bowl and mix well. Once combined, stir in the fresh coriander. Rub this mixture under the skin of the chicken, then rub the remainder inside the cavity. Leave to marinate in the refrigerator for 1 hour.

3   Preheat the oven to 180°C (350°F), Gas Mark 4. Put the chicken into a roasting tin and roast for 1 hour 20 minutes, which will give you a perfect tandoori chicken. To check it is done, pierce the thigh with a skewer – the juices should run clear. If not, continue roasting until they do.

4   Transfer the chicken to a serving plate and let it rest for 15 minutes before serving.

Onion and Whole Spice Chicken Curry

SERVES 4

1 tablespoon sunflower
  oil
2 bay leaves
1 cinnamon stick
8 black peppercorns
8 cloves
4 green cardamom
  pods
6 onions, 3 finely
  chopped, 3 quartered
2 small green chillies,
  finely chopped
2 garlic cloves, finely
  chopped
1 cm (½ inch) piece
  of fresh root ginger,
  peeled and finely
  chopped
2 tablespoons tomato
  purée
1 tablespoon ground
  coriander
1 teaspoon garam
  masala
1 teaspoon ground
  turmeric
1 teaspoon salt
100 ml (3½ fl oz)
  natural yogurt
100 ml (3½ fl oz)
  boiling water
8 skinless chicken
  thighs on the bone

This one is my go-to recipe for making the best chicken curry in the shortest amount of time, with the least amount of effort! It will soon be your favourite, too – the spices work their magic on the chicken, and the generous use of onions gives the dish a delicious flavour. Despite the fact that it's on my list of all-time top comfort foods, this meal is very healthy. Serve it with rice or chapatti.

1 Heat the oil in a saucepan over a medium–low heat. Once hot, add the bay leaves, cinnamon, peppercorns, cloves and cardamom and let them sizzle for a few seconds. Stir in the finely chopped onions and chillies and cook until the onions are golden brown – this might take 20–25 minutes.

2 Add the garlic and ginger to the saucepan and mix well. Continue to cook for 2 minutes, then stir in the tomato purée and cook for 2 minutes more. Now mix in the coriander, garam masala, turmeric and salt and cook for another minute.

3 Stir the yogurt into the saucepan along with the measured boiling water, then add the chicken and the quartered onions. Cover the pan with a lid and simmer gently for 40–45 minutes or until the chicken is cooked through. Serve immediately.

Coconut Chicken Curry

SERVES 4
1 ½ tablespoons
  sunflower oil
1 teaspoon mustard
  seeds
10 curry leaves
2 onions, thinly sliced
2 green chillies, thinly
  sliced
4 garlic cloves, finely
  chopped
1 cm (½ inch) piece
  of fresh root ginger,
  peeled and finely
  chopped
1 teaspoon salt
1 teaspoon ground
  turmeric
1 teaspoon ground
  coriander
½ teaspoon ground
  cinnamon
8 skinless chicken
  pieces on the bone
  (I use 4 thighs and 4
  drumsticks)
400 ml (14 fl oz) can
  coconut milk

So different to the heavily spiced chicken curries you may have tried, this dish has a delicate and refreshing flavour that's best enjoyed with rice rather than bread. The light spicing works beautifully with the coconut milk, and using chicken on the bone adds extra flavour. Don't save this luxurious-tasting curry for the weekend – being quick to make, it's a great choice for midweek meals.

1 Heat the oil in a saucepan over a medium–low heat. Stir in the mustard seeds and cook for 1–2 minutes, until they start to sizzle. Now mix in the curry leaves and, after 1 minute, add the onions and green chillies. Reduce the heat to low and cook for 5–6 minutes, until the onions have softened. Stir in the garlic and ginger and cook for another 2 minutes.

2 Add the salt and spices to the saucepan and mix well. Cook for 1 minute, then stir in the chicken, increase the heat to high and cook for 5 minutes, until the chicken is sealed.

3 Stir in the coconut milk, then cover the pan with a lid, reduce the heat to low and cook for 35–40 minutes, until the chicken is cooked through. Serve immediately.

Chicken Seekh Kebabs

SERVES 8

500 g (1 lb 2 oz)
  skinless chicken
  breast fillets
4 garlic cloves
1 cm (½ inch) piece
  of fresh root ginger,
  peeled
2 small green chillies
30 g (1 oz) fresh
  coriander
1 red onion, roughly
  chopped
¾ teaspoon salt
1 teaspoon Kashmiri
  chilli powder
½ teaspoon garam
  masala
½ teaspoon chaat
  masala
¼ teaspoon freshly
  ground black pepper
30 g (1 oz) Cheddar
  cheese, finely grated
2 tablespoons
  sunflower oil

These beautifully spiced and herby kebabs are great cooked over a barbecue, but can also be done in an oven or on a griddle pan, which is how I usually cook them. And you can shape the mixture into burgers to serve in a bun, if you prefer. Whatever shape or method you choose, the result will be the same – tender and delectable. Serve them on their own, or in a chapatti with chutney and salad.

1 If using bamboo skewers, soak 8 skewers in water for 30 minutes prior to cooking.

2 Using a food processor, break down the chicken breasts to a smooth paste, then tip the paste into a bowl.

3 Now put the garlic, ginger, chillies, coriander and onion into the bowl of the food processor and pulse to roughly chop and combine them. Add this mixture, along with the salt, dried spices, pepper and grated cheese, to the bowl with the minced chicken and mix thoroughly.

TO SERVE
(OPTIONAL)

red onion slices
2 tablespoons chopped
    fresh coriander
chilli flakes
lime wedges
natural yogurt
    sprinkled with
    toasted cumin seeds

4 Divide the mixture into 8 equal portions. Press 1 portion
   around a skewer, then roll it between your hands to give
   it a somewhat cylindrical shape and extend it along the
   skewer. Keep a bowl of water nearby to dip your hands
   into between shaping each skewer, as this makes it easier
   to handle the somewhat sticky mixture. Place the prepared
   skewer on a tray or chopping board and repeat the process
   with the remaining portions of the chicken mixture and
   skewers. If necessary, you can leave the kebabs to rest in the
   refrigerator for up to 24 hours until you are ready to cook.

5 Heat the oil in a griddle pan. Cook the kebabs over a
   medium–low heat for 8–10 minutes, turning halfway,
   until cooked through. Serve immediately with the red
   onion slices, chopped coriander, chilli flakes, lime wedges
   to squeeze over and cumin yogurt, if liked.

Chicken Chop

MAKES 20
1 tablespoon sunflower
  oil, plus extra for
  deep-frying
1 onion, finely
  chopped
1 small green chilli,
  finely chopped
2 garlic cloves, finely
  chopped
2.5 cm (1 inch) piece
  of fresh root ginger,
  peeled and finely
  chopped
1 teaspoon salt
½ teaspoon ground
  coriander
½ teaspoon ground
  cumin
1 teaspoon garam
  masala
500 g (1 lb 2 oz)
  minced chicken
2 boiled potatoes,
  peeled and mashed
handful of fresh
  coriander leaves,
  finely chopped
2 eggs, lightly beaten
100 g (3 ½ oz) golden
  breadcrumbs
coriander and spinach
  or tomato chutney,
  to serve

I really enjoyed eating these delicious hot snacks in Kolkata and was fascinated to see that the chefs give each flavour of chop a different shape – egg chops are oval, fish chops, cylindrical, and chicken chops are flat. It makes it very easy to tell them apart.

1 Heat the 1 tablespoon sunflower oil in a saucepan over a medium heat. Add the onion and chilli and cook for 5 minutes, until the onion softens. Add the garlic and ginger and cook for 2 minutes, then add the salt and spices and mix well. Stir in the minced chicken and remove the pan from the heat – you don't want to cook the chicken at this stage or it will not bind well.

2 Transfer the chicken mixture to a bowl. Add the mashed potatoes and coriander and mix well.

3 Divide the chicken mixture into 20 portions. Take 1 portion in your palm and shape it into an oval. Press gently to flatten it a little. Dip the patty in the beaten egg, then roll it in breadcrumbs until coated. Repeat until you've used up all the chicken mixture.

4 Fill a deep-fat fryer or large, heavy-based saucepan with enough oil for deep-frying. Slowly heat the oil to 190°C (375°F). Line a plate with some kitchen paper. When the oil is hot, fry the chicken chops, a few at a time, for 2–3 minutes, turning halfway through, until golden brown. Transfer to the paper-lined plate and leave to drain excess oil while you cook the remaining chicken chops. Serve hot with chutney.

Fish Fry

SERVES 2–4
½ teaspoon salt
½ teaspoon ground
turmeric
¼ teaspoon chilli
powder
1 medium sea bream,
cleaned, gutted and
cut into 6 pieces
2 handfuls of fresh
coriander leaves,
finely chopped
4 garlic cloves, finely
chopped
2 small green chillies,
finely chopped
4 tablespoons mustard
oil
2 tablespoons lemon
juice

This crispy, flavourful fried fish dish is a staple in Kolkata, where it's an essential part of the local thali and is eaten with lentils, potato and rice as a main meal, but it also makes a great snack. Coriander and garlic balance the peppery taste of the mustard oil in which the fish is fried.

1 Mix the salt, turmeric and chilli powder in a small bowl. Rub the spice mixture over the fish pieces, then put them into a bowl and leave to stand for 15 minutes.

2 Using a pestle and mortar, mash the coriander, garlic and green chilli to a paste. Smear it over the fish.

3 Heat the mustard oil in a frying pan set over medium heat. Just as it begins to smoke, add the fish pieces and cook for 2–3 minutes on each side, until golden and crisp. Sprinkle over the lemon juice. Serve immediately.

Amritsar-Style Fish

SERVES 4

sunflower oil, for
  shallow-frying
1 trout, about 400–
  500 g (14 oz–1 lb
  2 oz), cleaned, gutted
  and cut into 8 steaks
  about 1 cm (½ inch)
  thick

FOR THE BATTER

50 g (1¾ oz) gram
  flour (besan)
35 g (1¼ oz) plain
  flour
35 g (1¼ oz) cornflour
2 garlic cloves, grated
2.5 cm (1 inch) piece
  of fresh root ginger,
  peeled and grated
1 teaspoon carom
  seeds (ajwain)
½ teaspoon salt
½ teaspoon chilli
  powder
½ teaspoon ground
  turmeric
about 150 ml (¼ pint)
  water

TO SERVE

lime wedges
sliced red onion
chilli flakes

There are many delicious ways in which fish is cooked in Amritsar in North India, and when I visited the city a few years ago I fell in love with the local food. This recipe is inspired by a dish I ate there in a dhabba (small street-side restaurant), and even though it is simple, it's still so delicious. If you can't find trout, then feel free to use any other firm white fish. This is great served with some coriander chutney.

1 To make the batter, mix together all the ingredients except the measured water in a bowl. Then gradually whisk in enough of the water to make a smooth batter with a coating consistency.

2 Heat enough oil for shallow-frying in a frying pan. Line a plate with kitchen paper.

3 Wash the fish pieces and pat them dry. Dip one piece at a time into the batter and then carefully add to the hot oil. Cook over a medium–low heat for 2–3 minutes on each side until golden and cooked through. Transfer to the paper-lined plate to absorb the excess oil.

4 Serve with lime wedges and sliced red onion, sprinkled with chilli flakes.

Tamarind Fish Curry

SERVES 4

700 g (1 lb 9 oz) cod
  fillet, cut into 2–3 cm
  (¾–1¼ inch) pieces
¼ teaspoon salt
¼ teaspoon ground
  turmeric
fresh coconut, very
  finely chopped, to
  garnish (optional)

FOR THE SAUCE
1 tablespoon mustard
  oil
1 teaspoon mustard
  seeds
10 curry leaves
3 shallots, ground to
  a paste using a mini
  food processor
1 teaspoon fresh root
  ginger paste (made
  using a mini food
  processor or pestle
  and mortar)
1 teaspoon garlic paste
  (made using a mini
  food processor or
  pestle and mortar)
1 teaspoon ground
  coriander
½ teaspoon ground
  turmeric
½ teaspoon salt
1 tablespoon tamarind
  paste
400 ml (14 fl oz) can
  coconut milk

Cooking fish is such a joy – it's often a quick and easy job, and you can get so many different results from the same species. The layers of flavour in this curry are wonderful. The simple sauce is quick to produce, but it combines with the fish into something really special. Serve this dish with rice.

1 Put the cod into a large bowl and rub the pieces with the salt and turmeric. Cover the bowl with clingfilm and refrigerate until the curry sauce is almost ready.

2 To make the curry sauce, heat the oil in a saucepan over a medium heat. When it is smoking hot, add the mustard seeds and curry leaves. After 1–2 minutes, once they start to pop, stir in the shallot paste and cook for 3–5 minutes, until golden. Add the ginger and garlic pastes and cook for 1 minute, then stir in the coriander, turmeric and salt. Once combined, add the tamarind paste and coconut milk. Mix well, then cover the pan with a lid and cook for 8–10 minutes, until the sauce has thickened slightly.

3 Add the fish pieces to the sauce and cook gently for 3–4 minutes, until the fish is cooked through. Garnish with the fresh coconut, if liked, and serve immediately.

Fish and Lentil Curry

2 tablespoons rapeseed oil

1 teaspoon black mustard seeds

1 large red onion, finely chopped

2.5 cm (1 inch) piece of fresh root ginger, peeled and grated

2 tomatoes, finely chopped

1 teaspoon salt

2 teaspoons curry powder

1 teaspoon ground turmeric

1 teaspoon chilli powder

150 g (5½ oz) masoor dal (split red lentils)

400 ml (14 fl oz) can coconut milk

100 ml (3½ fl oz) boiling water

400 g (14 oz) skinless hake fillet or any firm white fish, cut into pieces 7.5 cm (3 inches) long

chopped chives, to serve

Fish in any curry is delicious but when cooked with lentils it makes for a wonderfully creamy and hearty dish. I asked my fishmonger which fish he suggested I cook in this curry and he gave me this lovely hake. It worked a treat, but any other firm white fish fillet would be lovely. Serve with Vegetable Pulao or plain rice.

1 Heat the oil in a pan and add the mustard seeds. Once they start to sizzle, add the onion and cook over a medium heat for 5 minutes until softened and starting to change colour. Then add the ginger and cook for a minute.

2 Add the tomatoes and cook over a medium heat for 2 minutes until they start to soften.

3 Stir in the salt and ground spices and then the lentils. Pour in the coconut milk followed by the measured boiling water. Cover and cook over a low–medium heat for 10 minutes until the lentils are soft.

4 Place the fish pieces in the lentils, cover again and cook over a medium heat for 5 minutes until the fish is just cooked through.

5 Sprinkle with chopped chives and serve.

Tandoori Pan-Fried Sea Bream

SERVES 2
1 whole sea bream
   (500 g–600 g/ 1 lb
   2 oz–1 lb 5 oz)
100 ml (3½ fl oz)
   natural yogurt
1 cm (½ inch) piece
   of fresh root ginger,
   peeled and finely
   chopped
1 tablespoon tandoori
   masala powder
½ teaspoon chilli
   powder
½ teaspoon salt
40 g (1½ oz) fresh
   coriander, leaves and
   stems finely chopped
2 teaspoons mustard
   oil

FOR THE GARNISH
handful of fresh
   coriander leaves
1 large red chilli, sliced
3 limes, halved or
   quartered, for
   squeezing over

The spices, fresh herbs and yogurt in this dish make it next-level tasty. When you are short on time but still want to cook up a feast, this dish is the best thing you can try – it could not be any simpler! The bream is good-looking enough to sit in the middle of any dining table, and is great served with salads, rice, bread or even on its own.

1 First, score 2 cuts across each side of the fish. Place it in a large dish.

2 In a bowl, combine the yogurt, ginger, tandoori masala, chilli powder, salt, coriander and 1 teaspoon of the mustard oil. Mix well, then spoon some of the mixture into the cavity of the fish. Spread the remainder over the outside of the fish. Leave to rest in the refrigerator for 10 minutes.

3 Heat the remaining mustard oil in a large frying pan over a medium heat. Once it is smoking hot, carefully lay the fish in the pan and cook for 5–6 minutes on each side or until the fish is cooked through and flaky.

4 Serve immediately on a large plate garnished with the coriander leaves, chilli slices and lime pieces.

Hot and Spicy Coconut Prawns

12 raw king prawns,
  shelled and deveined

FOR THE DRY RUB
1 cm (½ inch) piece
  of fresh root ginger,
  peeled and grated
2 garlic cloves, grated
¼ teaspoon salt
¼ teaspoon chilli
  powder
¼ teaspoon ground
  turmeric
¼ teaspoon crushed
  fennel seeds

FOR THE MASALA
1 tablespoon sunflower
  oil
10 curry leaves
½ teaspoon black
  mustard seeds
½ teaspoon fennel seeds
2 small green chillies,
  thinly sliced
2 red onions, thinly
  sliced
100 g (3½ oz) fresh
  coconut, thinly sliced

I'm warning you – this is a hot one! But, of course, you can reduce the quantity of chillies to suit your taste. The fresh prawns and big pieces of coconut are a match made in heaven. Curry leaves and fennel seeds also help to give this dish a unique flavour. Perhaps best of all, it comes together in minutes, making this a great quick-meal option. Serve it with some plain rice or pulao.

1   Put the prawns into a bowl with all the dry rub ingredients and rub them thoroughly over the prawns. Cover the bowl and leave to rest in the refrigerator for 15 minutes while you prepare the masala.

2   Heat the oil in a large saucepan over a medium heat. Add the curry leaves and the mustard and fennel seeds and let them sizzle for a few seconds. Now stir in the green chillies and onions and cook for 2–3 minutes, until they begin to soften.

150 ml (¼ pint)
  boiling water
½ teaspoon salt
½ teaspoon ground
  turmeric
½ teaspoon garam
  masala
1 teaspoon ground
  coriander
1 tablespoon Kashmiri
  chilli powder

3 Add the coconut to the saucepan along with the measured
   boiling water. Stir well, then cover the pan with a lid and
   cook for 10 minutes, until the coconut is slightly softer.

4 Next, add the salt, spices and prawns to the pan and
   mix gently. Increase the heat to high and cook for
   5–6 minutes, until the prawns have turned pink and are
   cooked through. Serve immediately.

Egg and Cabbage Curry

FOR THE CURRY
2 tablespoons rapeseed
    oil
2 dried bay leaves
2 onions, thinly sliced
½ hispi cabbage,
    about 200 g (7 oz),
    thinly sliced
1 teaspoon sugar
1 teaspoon salt
1 teaspoon chilli
    powder
1 teaspoon garam
    masala
½ teaspoon ground
    turmeric
200 ml (7 fl oz) boiling
    water

FOR THE EGGS
8 eggs
4 tablespoons double
    cream
2 tablespoons rapeseed
    oil

You may not have expected to find a recipe for egg curry in this chapter. I've put it here because many Hindus in India (most of whom are vegetarian) consider eggs to be a form of meat. There are so many ways of making this irresistible curry and I have shared a few versions of it over the years. The addition of cabbage in this recipe gives it a lovely texture and the egg yolks contribute an extra layer of flavour to the sauce. Serve with rice or spiced layered flatbread.

1 To make the curry, heat the oil in a pan, add the bay leaves and onions and cook over a high heat for about 5 minutes. Then add the cabbage and sugar and cook over a medium heat for 10 minutes until the vegetables are soft and golden. Stir in the salt and spices and cook for a minute.

2 While the curry is cooking, put the eggs in a pan, cover with boiling water and cook for 10 minutes. Drain, cool under cold running water and shell them. Cut the eggs in half and separate the egg whites and yolks. Mash the egg yolks with the cream in a bowl. Heat the oil in a pan and fry the egg whites for a couple of minutes until golden.

3 Add the mashed yolks, fried egg whites and measured boiling water to the curry. Cover and cook over a medium heat for 5 minutes until everything has come together, then serve.

DALS

Dal Fry

SERES 4

FOR THE DAL
150 g (5½ oz) toor dal
(split pigeon peas)
50 g (1¾ oz) moong
dal (split mung
beans)
50 g (1¾ oz) chana dal
(split chickpeas)
1 litre (1¾ pints)
boiling water
1 teaspoon salt
1 teaspoon ground
turmeric

FOR THE FIRST
TADKA
1 tablespoon ghee
1 tablespoon sunflower
oil
1 teaspoon cumin
seeds
2 garlic cloves, finely
chopped
1 cm (½ inch) piece
of fresh root ginger,
peeled and finely
chopped
1 green chilli, finely
chopped
1 onion, finely
chopped
handful of fresh
coriander leaves,
finely chopped

You might have seen this dal dish on the menu of your local takeaway, and it's just as popular in India, where it is served at dhabas (small roadside eateries). What makes it so delicious is the double tadka – one is stirred through the cooked lentils and the other sits on top of the final dish, waiting for you to break into it and enjoy this delicious combination of three lentils.

1   To make the dal, put all three types of lentils into a saucepan and cover with the measured boiling water. Leave to soak for 1 hour. Stir in the salt and turmeric and cook over a medium–low heat for 40–45 minutes until the lentils are soft and mushy.

2   Make the first tadka towards the end of the cooking time for the dal. Heat the ghee and oil in a saucepan over a medium–low heat and add the cumin seeds. Once they begin to sizzle, add the garlic, ginger, chilli and onion and cook for 5–6 minutes until the onion begins to turn golden. Stir in the chopped coriander and mix well, then pour the tadka over the cooked dal in the saucepan and mix it in well. Transfer the dal to a serving bowl.

2 tablespoons ghee
2 garlic cloves, thinly
   sliced
4 red chillies, thinly
   sliced
8–10 fresh curry leaves

3 Now make the second tadka. Heat the ghee over a medium–
   low heat in the same pan you used to make the first tadka.
   Add the garlic and chillies and cook for a minute until
   they soften. Now mix in the curry leaves and let the tadka
   sizzle for a few seconds, then pour it over the dal and
   serve immediately.

Cumin Dal

SERVES 4

FOR THE LENTILS
300 g (10½ oz) moong
  dal (split mung beans)
1.2 litres (2 pints)
  water
1 teaspoon salt
½ teaspoon ground
  turmeric

FOR THE TADKA
1 tablespoon ghee
1 teaspoon cumin
  seeds
2 small green chillies,
  halved
10 fresh curry leaves
20 g (¾ oz) fresh
  coriander leaves,
  finely chopped

Turn to this when you're short on time and need something healthy, delicious and comforting. Moong dal takes very little time to cook and needs only the simplest tempering to make it perfect. I would happily eat this as a bowl of soup, but my kids love it with yogurt and chapatti.

1 Put the dal, measured water, salt and turmeric into a deep pan and bring to the boil. Simmer on a low heat for 20 minutes, until the lentils are soft and mushy.

2 To make the tadka, in a small pan, melt the ghee and add the cumin seeds. Once they start to sizzle, add the green chillies and curry leaves, then, a few seconds later, the coriander.

3 Immediately pour the tadka over the lentils and serve.

4 This will keep in an airtight container in the refrigerator for 4–5 days. Reheat before serving.

Masala Urad Dal

SERVES 4
250 g (9 oz) urad dal
  (whole black lentils)
1 litre (1¼ pints)
  water
1 teaspoon salt
1 teaspoon ground
  turmeric
1 tablespoon ghee
1 teaspoon cumin
  seeds
a pinch of asafoetida
1 onion, finely
  chopped
1 cm (½ inch) fresh
  ginger, peeled and
  finely chopped
2 garlic cloves, finely
  chopped
1 green chilli, finely
  chopped
2 tomatoes, finely
  chopped
20 g (¾ oz) fresh
  coriander leaves,
  finely chopped
¼ teaspoon freshly
  ground black pepper

This particular dal is a bit different from the others as it is
quite thick, which is why it's usually served with flatbreads
such as naan or chapatti rather than rice. My mum used to
serve it with crispy hot parathas and raita on the side.

1   Put the dal and measured water into a pan and leave to
    soak for 2 hours.

2   Add the salt and turmeric to the dal and bring to the boil.
    Cover and cook over a low heat for 35–40 minutes, until
    very soft – there won't be much liquid left by the time the
    lentils are done.

3   In a separate pan, heat the ghee and add the cumin seeds.
    Once they start to sizzle, add the asafoetida and onion
    and cook for 10 minutes over a medium heat until deep
    golden brown. Next, add the ginger, garlic and green
    chilli and cook for another 2 minutes.

4   Add the chopped tomatoes and cook for 5 minutes, until
    softened. Throw in the coriander and black pepper and
    mix well.

5   Tip the cooked dal into the onion and tomato mixture
    and serve warm.

6   Store in an airtight container in the refrigerator for 4–5
    days and reheat before serving.

Spinach and Coconut Dal

SERVES 4

FOR THE LENTILS
250 g (9 oz) toor dal
(split pigeon peas)
1.2 litres (2 pints)
water
1 ¼ teaspoons salt
1 teaspoons ground
turmeric

FOR THE SPINACH
1 tablespoon ghee
1 tablespoon urad dal
(whole black lentils)
1 teaspoon cumin
seeds
2 teaspoons coriander
seeds
½ teaspoon freshly
ground black pepper
4 dried red chillies
50 g (1 ¾ oz) fresh
coconut, roughly
chopped
200 g (7 oz) fresh
spinach
100 ml (3 ½ fl oz)
boiling water

FOR THE TADKA
1 teaspoon ghee
1 teaspoon black
mustard seeds
2 dried red chillies
a pinch of asafoetida

Spinach and lentils are a very typical combination and I have got a few ways to cook them together, but this particular recipe is special. It flavours the spinach with lovely spices and coconut, making the taste unique. You can eat a bowl of this on its own, or serve it with rice.

1 Start by combining the lentils, measured water, salt and turmeric in a pan and bringing them to the boil. Reduce the heat, then cover and cook for 40–45 minutes, until the lentils are soft.

2 To cook the spinach, heat the ghee in another pan and add the urad dal. Cook for 2 minutes over a low heat until slightly golden, then add the cumin seeds, coriander seeds, black pepper, dried red chillies and chopped coconut. Let it all sizzle for a minute.

3 Add the spinach and measured boiling water. Cover and cook over a low heat for 2 minutes, until the spinach has wilted. Transfer the mixture to a blender and blitz to a purée.

4 Tip the purée into the pan of cooked lentils and return to the boil.

5 For the tadka, heat the ghee in a small pan. Add the mustard seeds, dried red chillies and asafoetida and let them sizzle for a minute. Stir this mixture into the lentils and serve.

6 Store in an airtight container in the refrigerator for 2–3 days. Reheat well before serving.

Garlic and Tamarind Rasam

SERVES 4

FOR THE RASAM
12–14 garlic cloves,
  thinly sliced
½ teaspoon salt
½ teaspoon ground
  turmeric
200 ml (7 fl oz) water
1 tablespoon ghee
1 teaspoon cumin
  seeds
2 dried red chillies
¼ teaspoon black
  peppercorns
1 tablespoon tamarind
  paste
800 ml (27 fl oz)
  boiling water

FOR THE TADKA
1 tablespoon ghee
1 teaspoon black
  mustard seeds
10 fresh curry leaves
1 tablespoon dark
  muscovado sugar
½ teaspoon salt

I didn't realize how many varieties of rasam there are in South Indian cooking until I visited my friend Renushree, who told me all about them as she made this incredible version. To begin with, I wasn't sure about the quantity of garlic – 12 to 14 cloves! – but it's one of the most amazing dishes I've eaten. The sour tamarind bounces off the sweetness of the sugar, and the garlic isn't overwhelming but melt-in-your-mouth sweet. This is perfect for when you're feeling run down.

1 Put the garlic, salt and turmeric into a pan with measured water and bring to the boil. Cook over a low heat for 20 minutes, until the garlic is soft.

2 In a small pan, heat the ghee. Add the cumin seeds, dried chillies and peppercorns and fry for a few seconds, until golden. Crush this mixture with a pestle and mortar, then add it to the pan of garlic.

3 Add the tamarind paste and the measured boiling water to the garlic too, then continue to cook over low heat for 10 minutes so that all the flavours can infuse.

4 To make the tadka, heat the ghee in a small pan. Add the mustard seeds and when they start to pop, remove the pan from the heat and add the curry leaves, muscovado sugar and salt.

5 Pour this over the rasam and serve immediately in small heatproof glasses or bowls to drink straight up.

6 This will keep in an airtight container in the refrigerator for 4–5 days. It is best to bring it to a boil before serving but do try it cold as well.

Black Lentils with Red Kidney Beans

SERVES 4–6

300 g (10½ oz) urad dal
(whole black lentils)
100 g (3½ oz) dried
red kidney beans
roughly 500 ml
(18 fl oz) water,
for soaking
1.4 litres (2½ pints)
water
1½ teaspoons salt
4 black cardamom
pods
1 tablespoon ghee
4 garlic cloves, finely
chopped
1 small green chilli,
finely chopped
2 tablespoons tomato
purée
1 tablespoon garam
masala
1 teaspoon chilli
powder
100–200 ml (3½
–7 fl oz) boiling
water, to loosen, if
required
1 tablespoon double
cream

TO GARNISH
1 tablespoon chopped
fresh coriander
1 small green chilli,
thinly sliced

My kids tell me this is one of their favourite lentil dishes. Cooking it with love, slowly over a low heat, brings out the flavour of the black lentils and black cardamom and results in a rich, intense, deep taste. And the best part is that it tastes even better the next day, so be sure to make a little extra. Serve it with rice, naan or chapatti.

1 Soak the lentils and beans in the measured soaking water for 4–5 hours.

2 Transfer the pulses and their soaking water to a deep saucepan and add the measured water, plus the salt and black cardamom pods. Bring the liquid to the boil, then cover the pan with a lid and simmer over a low heat for 1 hour or until the lentils and beans are cooked.

3 In a separate large saucepan, heat the ghee over a low heat, then add the garlic and chilli and cook for 1 minute. Stir in the tomato purée, garam masala and chilli powder and cook for another minute.

4 Tip the cooked lentils and beans into the pan of spices, mixing well. Cover the pan with a lid and cook over a low heat for 1–1½ hours, stirring every 10–15 minutes to ensure the mixture does not stick to the base of the pan. If the lentils become too thick during cooking, add just enough of the measured boiling water to loosen the mixture.

5 Finally, when the dal is ready, add the cream and mix well. Garnish with the coriander and sliced chilli and serve immediately with rice, naan or chapatti.

Five Lentils

SERVES 4

100 g (3½ oz) moong
  dal (split mung beans)
100 g (3½ oz) chana
  dal (split chickpeas)
100 g (3½ oz) moong
  sabut (whole green
  mung beans)
50 g (1¾ oz) urad dal
  (whole black lentils)
50 g (1¾ oz) toor dal
  (split pigeon peas)
500 ml (18 fl oz) cold
  water, for soaking
1 teaspoon salt
500 ml (18 fl oz)
  boiling water
1 tablespoon chopped
  fresh coriander, to
  garnish (optional)

FOR THE
TEMPERING

1 tablespoon ghee
pinch of asafoetida
2.5 cm (1 inch) piece
  of fresh root ginger,
  peeled and julienned
1 onion, thinly sliced
1 small green chilli,
  thinly sliced
1 tomato, thinly sliced
½ teaspoon chilli
  powder
½ teaspoon ground
  cumin
½ teaspoon amchur
  (mango powder)
½ teaspoon salt

Each lentil variety in this extraordinary dish brings its
unique flavour, but feel free to skip one or two if you don't
have them all to hand – simply increase the quantities of
the others to fill the gap. The dish is deceptively simple to
make. It is the tempering (adding fried spices, onion, chilli
and other flavourings at the end of cooking) that gives it an
impressive colour boost and flavour kick. Serve the dal with
rice or chapatti.

1 Soak all the lentils together in the measured soaking
   water in a deep saucepan for 2–3 hours. When they have
   swollen, transfer the pan to the hob, stir in the salt and
   bring the mixture to the boil. Once boiling, half-cover
   the pan with a lid, reduce the heat to low and simmer for
   30 minutes. Once the cooking time has elapsed, add the
   measured boiling water to the pan and continue to cook
   for 30 minutes or until the lentils are soft.

2 Heat the ghee in a saucepan over a medium heat. Add
   the asafoetida. After a minute or so, when it starts to
   sizzle and smells fragrant, mix in the ginger and cook for
   1 minute. Next, stir in the onion and chilli and cook for
   4–5 minutes, until the onion is soft.

3 Stir the tomato slices into the onion mixture and cook for
   2 minutes, until they just begin to soften. Now add the
   chilli powder, cumin, amchur and salt, mix well and cook
   for 1 minute more.

4 Pour the lentils into a deep serving bowl and spoon
   the onion mixture over the top. Garnish with chopped
   coriander, if liked, and serve warm.

RICE & BREADS

Cumin Rice

SERVES 4
1 tablespoon sunflower
  oil
1 tablespoon ghee
2 teaspoons cumin
  seeds
1½ teaspoons salt
300 g (10½ oz)
  basmati rice, washed
  and drained
1 teaspoon ground
  cumin
1 teaspoon chilli
  powder
20 g (¾ oz) fresh
  coriander leaves,
  finely chopped
700 ml (1¼ pints)
  boiling water

As the name suggests, this dish has tons of cumin in it –
both whole and ground seeds – giving it a wonderful earthy,
comforting warmth. Try it as a simple rice accompaniment for
all the lovely curries in this book. To be honest, I'd happily
eat this rice with just some yogurt.

1 Heat the oil and ghee in a saucepan over a medium–low
   heat, then add the cumin seeds. Cook for a few seconds
   until they begin to sizzle. Stir in the salt, then add the rice
   and stir well. Next, add the spices and coriander, then
   the measured boiling water. Cover the pan with a lid and
   cook over a low heat for 15 minutes.

2 Once the cooking time has elapsed, turn off the heat but
   don't lift off the lid. Leave the rice to rest for 15 minutes
   before serving.

Peanut, Coriander and Lemon Rice

SERVES 4

2 tablespoons
   groundnut oil
60 g (2¼ oz) blanched
   peanuts
1 teaspoon mustard
   seeds
12–14 fresh curry
   leaves
1 onion, thinly sliced
2 green chillies, thinly
   sliced
handful of fresh
   coriander leaves,
   roughly chopped
1 teaspoon salt
1 teaspoon chilli
   powder
1 teaspoon ground
   turmeric
1 teaspoon ground
   cumin
300 g (10½ oz)
   basmati rice, washed
   and drained
grated zest and juice
   of 2 lemons
600 ml (20 fl oz)
   boiling water

This simple peanut-lemon rice with lots of coriander and curry leaves is seriously delicious. Because it is ready within minutes, it's perfect for when you need a substantial snack (have it with your favourite chutney), but it also makes a lovely accompaniment to any curry.

1 Heat the oil in a saucepan, then add the peanuts. Cook over a medium–low heat for 2 minutes until golden. Stir in the mustard seeds and curry leaves and let them sizzle for a few seconds, then mix in the onion and chillies. Cook for 5 minutes until they have softened.

2 Next, add the coriander, salt and spices to the pan and mix well. Now add the rice and stir until all the rice is coated well. Mix in the lemon zest and measured boiling water, cover the pan with a lid and cook over a low heat for 10 minutes until the rice is almost cooked.

3 Lift off the lid, pour in the lemon juice evenly across the top of the rice, then replace the lid and cook over a low heat for 5 minutes until the rice is fully cooked. Leave to rest without taking the lid off for about 10 minutes before serving.

Bengali Khichdi

130 g (4½ oz) moong
   dal (split mung beans)
130 g (4½ oz) basmati
   rice
500 ml (18 fl oz) water
1 tablespoon ghee
1 cinnamon stick
4 green cardamom
   pods
6 cloves
2 cm (¾ inch) fresh
   ginger, peeled and
   grated
1 teaspoon salt
½ teaspoon sugar
1 teaspoon ground
   turmeric
½ teaspoon chilli
   powder
2 tomatoes, roughly
   chopped
650 ml (22 fl oz)
   boiling water

FOR THE TADKA
1 tablespoon ghee
2 green chillies, thinly
   sliced
20 g (¾ oz) fresh
   coriander leaves,
   finely chopped

I enjoyed this stunning khichdi at the home of Ranjana, who runs a takeaway khichdi business in Delhi called Bhaat. It's a dish from her menu. I love that it's such a simple, one-pot meal – the sort of dish that's incredibly comforting to eat on a cold day – yet the flavours are truly amazing. All it needs is a side of raita.

1 Toast the moong dal in a dry pan over a low heat for 4–5 minutes, until it starts to change colour. Put it into a pan with the rice and rinse well, two or three times, with water. Drain, then soak the dal and rice in the measured water for an hour.

2 Heat the ghee in a large pan. Add the cinnamon, cardamom, cloves and ginger and cook for a minute over a low heat. Add the salt, sugar, turmeric and chilli powder and cook for a few seconds, then stir in the tomatoes.

3 Drain the dal and rice and add them to the pan. Cook, stirring, over a high heat for 2 minutes. Pour in the measured boiling water, then cover and cook over a low heat for 15 minutes, until the dal and rice are soft and squishy.

4 To make the tadka, melt the ghee in a small pan. Add the green chillies and let them sizzle for a few seconds, then add the coriander leaves. Pour the mixture over the khichdi and serve warm.

5 This can be stored in an airtight container in the refrigerator for 4–5 days. Heat thoroughly before serving.

Aubergine and Potato Rice

SERVES 4

FOR THE SPICE
MIX

2 tablespoons urad dal
(whole black lentils)
2 tablespoons
coriander seeds
1 tablespoon chana dal
(split chickpeas)
1 cinnamon stick
2 dried red chillies
6 cloves

FOR THE RICE

900 g (2 lb) cooked
basmati rice or 300 g
(10½ oz) uncooked
rice
2 tablespoons
sunflower oil
1 teaspoon black
mustard seeds
2 red onions, thinly
sliced
1 potato, halved
lengthways and cut
into 5 mm (¼ inch)
slices
1 large aubergine,
halved lengthways
and cut into 5 mm
(¼ inch) slices
1 teaspoon salt
½ teaspoon ground
turmeric

When you've got leftover rice in the refrigerator, this makes a fabulous one-pot meal that simply needs a dollop of raita to serve. In fact, it's wonderful even without the rice! Feel free to eat the aubergine and potato mixture with chapatti or naan.

1 If you have not already done so, boil the rice according to the packet instructions and drain if necessary.

2 To make the spice mix, put all the ingredients into a dry pan and toast on a low heat for 2 minutes, until they change colour. Leave to cool slightly, then grind to a powder using a small blender or a spice grinder.

3 Heat the oil in a large pan over a medium heat. Add the mustard seeds and, when they begin to sizzle, add the onions and cook for 5–7 minutes, until they start to change colour. Mix in the potato, then cover and cook over a low heat for 5 minutes – the potato will start to soften but should not be cooked through yet.

4 Add the aubergine slices, stir well, then cover and cook over a low heat for 10 minutes, until the potato and aubergine are fully cooked. Add your spice powder, plus the salt and turmeric, and cook over a low heat for 1 minute.

5 Finally, add the cooked rice and turn the heat to high. Stir until the rice and vegetables are well mixed and hot through, then serve.

6 Store in an airtight container in the refrigerator for 4–5 days. Reheat before serving.

Vegetable Pulao

SERVES 4

1 tablespoon sunflower
  oil
1 onion, finely
  chopped
6 spring onions, finely
  chopped
1 green pepper, finely
  chopped
2 tomatoes, finely
  chopped
150g (5½ oz) fresh or
  frozen peas
1 teaspoon salt
1 teaspoon garam
  masala
½ teaspoon ground
  turmeric
¼ teaspoon freshly
  ground black pepper
4 servings of cooked
  basmati rice

Made right in front of you on the streets of Mumbai, this
vegetarian pulao is super-delicious. In Mumbai they serve it
with potato curry, green chutney and a little raita, which is
a great combination, but you can also enjoy this satisfying
rice dish on its own.

1 Heat the oil in a saucepan over a medium heat. Add the
   onion and cook for about 5 minutes, until softened. Reserve
   a handful of the green parts of the spring onion for garnish
   and add the rest to the onion in the pan. Cook for 2
   minutes, until the spring onion begins to soften, then add
   the green pepper and tomatoes and mix well to combine.

2 If using frozen peas, blanch them in boiling water for
   2 minutes and drain before use. Add the fresh or blanched
   frozen peas to the onion, mix well and cook for 2 minutes,
   until well combined, then stir in the salt, garam masala,
   turmeric and black pepper.

3 Stir the cooked rice into the saucepan and cook for a final
   4–5 minutes, until the rice is heated through, then remove
   from the heat and serve hot, garnished with the reserved
   spring onion.

Quick Naan

MAKES 4

220 g (7 ¾ oz) self-
raising flour, plus
extra for dusting
¼ teaspoon salt
¼ teaspoon chilli
flakes
¼ teaspoon nigella
seeds
200 ml (7 fl oz) natural
yogurt
salted butter or ghee,
to serve

This is a super-simple and quick naan recipe. Adding baking powder and yogurt to the dough creates fluffy, pillowy naan breads that are ready in minutes. Once made, you can top the naan with garlic, chilli and coriander if you like.

1 Mix the flour, salt, chilli flakes and nigella seeds in a mixing bowl. Add the yogurt and mix well with your hands to form a dough. The dough may be slightly sticky at first, but continue to knead it for 2–3 minutes until it becomes a little smoother. Leave the dough in the bowl, cover the bowl with a clean tea towel and let the dough rest for 5 minutes.

2 Heat a frying pan or griddle pan over a medium heat. Divide the dough into 4 equal portions. Dust your work surface with a little flour, then roll out each dough portion into a circle with a diameter of 13–15 cm (5–6 inches). Cook in the hot pan for 1 minute on each side until golden.

3 Once cooked, brush each naan with butter or ghee and serve nice and hot.

Basic Chapatti

MAKES 12
300 g (10½ oz)
  chapatti flour, plus
  extra for dusting
roughly 175 ml
  (6 fl oz) water
ghee, to serve

There are many different recipes for making chapatti, but this is the way my family has made them for generations. Our version is a healthy one – there is no added salt, oil or any other ingredient, just flour and water, which gives you perfect, simple chapatti that taste amazing. Use them to scoop up sabjis, curries, chutneys and pickles, and as wraps.

1 Put the flour into a bowl. Very slowly, mix in just enough of the measured water to bring the mixture together in a dough – you might not need all the water or you may need a little more, so add just a few drops at a time. This is the best way to achieve a dough that is the correct consistency: smooth but not sticky.

2 Once the dough has come together, knead it on a clean surface for 2 minutes. Leave it to rest, either in a covered bowl or an airtight box, for 15–20 minutes.

3 Divide the dough into 12 equal portions. Roll each portion into a ball in your hands, then roll each ball in a little flour to dust. Using a rolling pin, roll out each ball into a circle with a diameter of 15–18 cm (6–7 inches).

4 Heat a skillet over a medium heat until hot. Carefully transfer one rolled-out portion of dough to the hot skillet and cook it for a few seconds on the first side, then turn. Allow the chapatti to bubble up a little on the second side, which will only take a few seconds, then turn it over again and cook for a few seconds, until it is golden and cooked through, pressing gently on the edges with some kitchen paper or a clean tea towel, which encourages the flatbread to puff up a little. Transfer the chapatti to a serving plate and spread a tiny amount of ghee across the top surface. Keep hot while you repeat the process with the remaining portions of dough. The best way to keep your chapatti soft and warm until serving is to wrap them in foil or in a clean tea towel until ready to eat. Serve the chapatti hot.

Parotha

MAKES 4

300 g (10½ oz) plain
  flour, plus extra for
  dusting
1 teaspoon salt
2 teaspoons caster
  sugar
100 ml (3½ fl oz) milk
approximately 150 ml
  (¼ pint) sunflower
  oil
80 ml (2¾ fl oz) water

These flatbreads are inspired by the famous Malabar parothas of Kerala. The dough is straightforward enough to make, but you do need to give it time to rest between the various steps, and you can't be stingy with the oil! This way, the dough relaxes, allowing the lovely flaky layers to appear. Indeed, it's these dreamy layers that make this special flatbread perfect for your Sunday feasts.

1 Mix together the dry ingredients in a large bowl. Stir in the milk and 1 tablespoon oil. Add the measured water a little at a time and, using your hand, bring the mixture together to form a soft dough. Knead for 5 minutes, then place the dough in the bowl, cover the bowl with a clean tea towel and set aside to rest for 30 minutes.

2 Divide the dough into 4 equal portions and shape them into balls. Drizzle 1 teaspoon oil over each dough ball to cover. Cover with the tea towel and leave to rest for 30 minutes.

3 Working with 1 dough ball at a time, roll out the ball on a lightly oiled work surface into a thin circle, then drizzle over 1 teaspoon oil and spread it over the dough circle. Using your fingers, stretch the dough into a circle with a diameter of 30–35 cm (12–14 inches). Spread another teaspoon of oil over the circle, then pick up one side of the circle and fold it like a fan, pinching it together until you have a long, gathered piece of dough. Twist this around your thumb to make a spiral (like a cinnamon roll), then tuck the tail of the dough into the centre of the spiral. Cover with the tea towel and leave to rest for 30 minutes.

4 Again working on 1 piece at a time, roll out the twisted dough ball into a circle with a diameter of roughly 20 cm (8 inches).

5 Heat a frying pan to a high heat and, once hot, cook 1 parotha for 1 minute on each side. Now drizzle 1 teaspoon oil over the paratha and turn it over to cook that side again for 1 minute until golden. Meanwhile, drizzle 1 teaspoon oil over the surface now facing up. Once the underside is golden, flip the parotha and cook for another minute until both sides are golden. Transfer the cooked parotha to a clean surface and, using your hands, push the edges in towards the centre, encouraging the layers to open up. Repeat the process to cook the remaining parothas. Serve immediately.

Gram Flour Roti

MAKES 8

200 g (7 oz) chapatti
flour, plus extra for
dusting
50 g (1 ¼ oz) gram
flour (besan)
½ teaspoon salt
½ teaspoon ground
turmeric
½ teaspoon chilli
powder
2 tablespoons kasuri
methi (dried
fenugreek leaves)
1 tablespoon oil
120 ml (4 fl oz) water,
plus extra if needed
ghee

This is inspired by a traditional Gujarati flatbread called
thepla, originally from western India but now popular all
over the world – and with good reason! It's easy, versatile
and delicious. My version makes it healthy as well. Serve it
with anything you like, or just with some chutney.

1 Combine all the dry ingredients in a bowl. Mix in the oil,
   then gradually add just enough of the water (or a little
   more if necessary) to form a soft dough. Knead in the
   bowl for a couple of minutes or until smooth, then cover
   and leave to rest for 30 minutes.

2 Divide the dough into 8 equal portions. Taking one at
   a time, roll out on a lightly floured surface to a circle
   roughly 18 cm (7 inches) wide.

3 Heat a flat griddle or pan over a low–medium heat and,
   once hot, cook each roti for 1–2 minutes. Turn and cook
   for another minute on the other side, then remove to a
   plate. Brush a little ghee on top and serve warm.

4 The dough will keep in an airtight container in the
   refrigerator for 2–3 days.

Rava Dosa

MAKES 4

120 g (4¼ oz) semolina
120 g (4¼ oz) rice flour
60 g (2¼ oz) plain
    flour
1 teaspoon salt
½ teaspoon chilli
    powder
1 teaspoon cumin
    seeds
¼ teaspoon freshly
    ground black pepper
1 red onion, finely
    chopped
2.5 cm (1 inch) piece
    of fresh root ginger,
    peeled and finely
    chopped
10 fresh curry leaves,
    finely chopped
handful of fresh
    coriander leaves
    and stems, finely
    chopped
1 tablespoon natural
    yogurt
900 ml (1½ pints)
    water
sunflower oil, for
    cooking

This light and crispy type of dosa, made with rava (semolina), is quick to make compared with normal dosa, for which you need a few days for fermenting the rice and lentils. Rava dosas provide the perfect quick meal that still feels like a huge treat. Serve them with a bowl of dal or some coconut chutney for a feast with delicious South Indian flavours.

1   Put all the ingredients, except the water and oil, into a large bowl and mix well. Now add half the measured water and whisk until smooth. Add the remaining water and whisk again. Cover the bowl and set the mixture aside to rest for 30 minutes.

2   Heat a frying pan until it is smoking hot. Put a few drops of oil in the pan, then wipe them away with a sheet of kitchen paper so that the pan is clean. Now ladle in the batter in a large circle, adding just enough to create a thin layer with some holes in it. These are characteristic of rava dosa, so don't fill them up with more batter. Drizzle 1 teaspoon oil all around the edges of the dosa and cook over a medium heat for roughly 2 minutes until the dosa is golden and crispy. Fold in half and serve immediately. Continue cooking the rest of the dosa batter in the same way.

Masala Puri

MAKES 20

300 g (10½ oz) chapati flour, plus extra for dusting

½ teaspoon salt

½ teaspoon chilli powder

½ teaspoon ground turmeric

1 teaspoon ground coriander

1 teaspoon carom seeds (ajwain)

approximately 220–240 ml (7½–8½ fl oz) water

sunflower oil, for deep-frying

Puri is a very popular type of bread in India and is often enjoyed at festivals, weddings and other special occasions. The dough is similar to chapati dough, but for this recipe I have added some lovely spices to it. The joy comes from deep-frying the dough until it puffs up. Puris are amazing served hot, but are often taken cold on picnics and train journeys in India to eat with some dry sabji (vegetable curry).

1 Put the flour, salt and spices into a bowl and mix well. Now slowly add just enough of the measured water (or more, if necessary) to bring the mixture together into a soft dough. Knead the dough for 2 minutes, then leave the dough in the bowl, cover the bowl with a clean tea towel and set aside to rest for 15–30 minutes.

2 Divide the dough into 20 equal portions and shape these into small balls. Working on a lightly floured surface, roll them out into thin circles with a diameter of roughly 7.5 cm (3 inches).

3 Heat enough oil for deep-frying in a deep, heavy-based saucepan or deep-fat fryer to 170–180°C (340–350°F). (Maintain this temperature range throughout cooking.) Gently place 1 puri into the oil and let it puff up. After 1 minute, turn it over in the oil and cook for another minute. Using a slotted spoon, remove the puri from the oil and transfer it to a bowl. Cook the remaining puris one at a time in this way. Serve immediately.

CHUTNEYS & SIDES

Mango Chutney

SERVES 6–8

2 tablespoons
  sunflower oil
1 teaspoon nigella
  seeds
4 garlic cloves, finely
  chopped
1 cm (½ inch) piece
  of fresh root ginger,
  peeled and finely
  chopped
3 red chillies, finely
  chopped
½ teaspoon salt
¼ teaspoon ground
  turmeric
¼ teaspoon ground
  cinnamon
¼ teaspoon ground
  cardamom
¼ teaspoon ground
  cumin
¼ teaspoon ground
  coriander
2 large mangoes,
  peeled, stoned and
  cut into 1–2 cm
  (½–¾ inch) pieces
150 g (5½ oz) caster
  sugar
3 tablespoons white
  vinegar

There are so many snacks this chutney works well with, and it's also great in sandwiches, salads and much more. I'm not the biggest fan of sweet chutneys – I like them with a bit of spice and a kick of chilli – so while this chutney certainly ticks the sweet box, it is vibrant and alive.

1 Heat the oil in a saucepan over a medium–low heat, then add the nigella seeds. Cook for a few seconds until they begin to sizzle, then stir in the garlic, ginger and chillies and let them cook for a few seconds. Now add the salt and spices, followed by the mangoes, and mix well, then stir in the sugar. Next, add the vinegar and mix well, then cover the pan with a lid and cook over a low heat for 50–60 minutes, stirring occasionally, until the mangoes have softened and the chutney has thickened. Leave to cool completely before serving.

2 Store in an airtight container in the refrigerator for up to 2 weeks.

Garlic Pickle

MAKES ROUGHLY
250 G (9 OZ)

40 garlic cloves, peeled
2 tablespoons mustard
  oil
10 small green
  chillies, quartered
  lengthways
1 teaspoon salt
1 teaspoon chilli
  powder
1 teaspoon ground
  turmeric
1 tablespoon grated
  or roughly chopped
  jaggery

FOR THE SPICE
BLEND

2 teaspoons fenugreek
  seeds
2 teaspoons black
  mustard seeds
2 teaspoons cumin
  seeds
2 teaspoons coriander
  seeds

Almost any Indian dish can be paired with this delicious, strongly flavoured pickle, which has a pleasing smoky hint and a good chilli hit. Whether you serve it alongside lentils, chicken, fish or veg, it's bound to make the meal more special.

1 First, make the spice blend. Heat a dry frying pan over a low heat. Add the seeds and toast them for about 2 minutes, until they are fragrant and you can see them starting to smoke – but don't let them colour or burn! Use a pestle and mortar to grind the toasted seeds to a rough powder. Set aside.

2 Chop any really large garlic cloves lengthways into smaller pieces so that all the pieces of garlic are of a similar size.

3 Heat the oil in a saucepan over a low heat. When it is smoking hot, add the garlic and green chillies and cook for 5–7 minutes, until the garlic begins to soften but doesn't colour.

4 Add the spice blend along with the salt, chilli powder, turmeric and jaggery. Mix well and cook for 2 minutes, until the jaggery has melted.

5 Spoon the mixture into a sterilized jar and seal well. Leave the pickle to mature in a warm place for 1 week before serving. Once the jar is open, it will keep well in the refrigerator for up to 3 months.

Mango and Mint Chutney

100 g (3½ oz) green
  or unripe mango,
  peeled and diced
40 g (1½ oz) mint,
  leaves picked
40 g (1½ oz) fresh
  coriander
½ teaspoon salt
½ teaspoon sugar
2 small green chillies
1 tablespoon lime juice
4 tablespoons water

I love a good, herby, fresh green chutney and this one goes
with almost any meal you might cook from this book. Using
green mango adds a tangy flavour and a lovely summery
note. If you can't find any small green mangoes, go for a big,
really hard, unripe mango from the supermarket, which will
work just as well.

1 Put all the ingredients into the bowl of a mini food
   processor. Whizz until smooth. Serve immediately.

2 This chutney will keep in an airtight container in the
   refrigerator for 4–5 days.

Carrot and Onion Pickle

MAKES ROUGHLY
600 G (1 LB 5 OZ)

2 carrots, cut into
  strips
2 red onions, thinly
  sliced
12 small green chillies,
  thinly sliced
2 pieces of fresh
  turmeric, peeled and
  thinly sliced
1 teaspoon salt
½ teaspoon chilli
  powder
2 teaspoons black
  mustard seeds,
  lightly crushed
150 ml (¼ pint) cider
  vinegar

You'll love this crunchy, fresh and spicy pickle. Serve it with any of the dishes in this book, but it's especially good with rice and lentils.

1 Mix all the ingredients together in a large bowl, ensuring they are well combined.

2 Pack the mixture into a sterilized jar and leave in a dark place for 24 hours. Transfer the jar to the refrigerator after that, where it will keep for 7–10 days.

Spinach Raita

SERVES 4

FOR THE RAITA
1 teaspoon sunflower
  oil
1 teaspoon cumin
  seeds
200 g (7 oz) fresh
  spinach leaves, finely
  chopped
200 g (7 oz) natural
  yogurt
¼ teaspoon salt
¼ teaspoon ground
  cumin

FOR THE TADKA
1 teaspoon sunflower
  oil
1 teaspoon black
  mustard seeds
1 garlic clove, finely
  chopped
2 dried red chillies
10 fresh curry leaves

I would be happy with just a bowl of this on its own – the garlic, curry leaves and chilli in the tadka taste amazing when added to the spinach yogurt. I tried this for the first time at my friend, Pranoti's house. She makes it often to serve with meals. You'll find it's great with any curry, in a wrap, with rice or bread – a real all-rounder.

1   To start the raita, heat the oil in a pan and add the cumin seeds. Once they start to sizzle, add the spinach leaves and cook, stirring, for 2 minutes on a high heat until the leaves have wilted and softened. Remove from the heat and leave to cool slightly.

2   In a bowl, combine the yogurt, salt and ground cumin, and stir in the wilted spiced spinach.

3   To make the tadka, heat the oil in a small pan and add the mustard seeds. Once they start to sizzle, add the garlic, dried red chillies and curry leaves and cook for a few seconds. Pour this into the raita, mix and serve.

Coriander and Mint Chutney

**MAKES A
SMALL BOWL**

100 g (3 ½ oz) fresh
  coriander
100 g (3 ½ oz) fresh
  mint leaves
2 green chillies
juice of 1 lime
1 teaspoon salt
½ teaspoon sugar
3 tablespoons water

I've shared a coriander chutney in every book I've written, but it really is amazing and key to my kitchen: I have a jar of it in my refrigerator at all times and it will last three or four days. You can also freeze this in small portions, and simply take out to defrost as and when needed.

1 Put all the ingredients into a blender, grind to a smooth paste and serve.

Tamarind and Date Chutney

MAKES A SMALL
BOWL

50 g (1¾ oz) tamarind
  pulp
50 g (1¾ oz) pitted
  dates
50 g (1¾ oz) jaggery
350 ml (12 fl oz) water
½ teaspoon salt
1 teaspoon ground
  cumin
1 teaspoon chilli
  powder
1 teaspoon ground
  ginger
1 teaspoon toasted
  fennel seeds, lightly
  crushed

Another of the chutneys I really can't do without! I make a big jar of this and keep it in the refrigerator to use over the course of six weeks or so. It's great when served with canapés, snacks, at barbecues and much more – a classic that will never go out of fashion.

1 Combine the tamarind, dates, jaggery and measured water in a pan. Bring to the boil, then reduce the heat to low and cook for 15–20 minutes.

2 Strain the mixture through a fine sieve into a jug, making sure you press down well on the ingredients to extract maximum flavour.

3 Return the sieved mixture in the jug to the pan and add the salt, cumin, chilli powder, ginger and fennel seeds. Cook gently for 2 minutes, then leave to cool before storing it in a jar.

SWEET
THINGS

Almond Halwa

100 g (3½ oz) unsalted
  butter or ghee
140 g (5 oz) ground
  almonds
140 ml (4¾ fl oz) milk
¼ teaspoon ground
  cardamom
pinch of saffron
  threads
40 g (1½ oz) golden
  caster sugar
handful of pistachio
  nuts, crushed

Halwa is one of the easiest Indian desserts to cook, and the ingredients are versatile – you can use nuts, semolina, lentils or flour. The almond version is usually made by soaking the whole nuts overnight, then peeling them, drying them and grinding them to a powder. I make the process quicker and easier by using ready-ground almonds – much less work for all the taste! Use ghee to cook this dish if you can – the flavours and oils released are delicious.

1 Heat the butter or ghee in a saucepan over a medium heat. Once it begins to bubble and sizzle, add the ground almonds and reduce the heat to low. Cook for 12–14 minutes, stirring every 2 minutes, until the mixture turns a deep golden colour.

2 Meanwhile, pour the milk into a jug, add the cardamom and saffron and stir well to combine. Set aside.

3 Add the sugar to the almond mixture in the pan and mix well. Continue to cook over a low heat for 2 minutes, stirring continuously to encourage the sugar to dissolve. Once the sugar has dissolved, slowly pour in the spiced milk, stirring continuously until the milk is incorporated. Now cook for 3–4 minutes until the mixture thickens. Take the pan off the heat, then sprinkle the crushed pistachios on top. Serve warm.

Walnut and Hazelnut Laddoos

MAKES 15
85 g (3 oz) walnuts
85 g (3 oz) hazelnuts
150 g (5½ oz) chapatti
  flour
3 tablespoons ghee
3 tablespoons agave
  nectar
1 teaspoon ground
  cardamom
¼ teaspoon rose water
dried rose petals,
  to decorate

Nuts add such a lovely flavour to these laddoos, and also help to bind them so they hold their shape well. Quick and simple to make, these tempting treats are scented with cardamom and also rose water, which adds a delicate, heart-warming floral touch. Laddoos are a great sweet with which to end a meal, but I warn you – it is difficult to stop at just one.

1 Put the nuts into a dry frying pan over a medium–low heat and toast them, stirring continuously, for 5 minutes or until they change colour.

2 Tip the toasted nuts into a mini food processor and blitz to a paste – keep blending until the nuts release their oil. Transfer the nut paste to a bowl.

3 Put the flour into the same dry frying pan and toast it over a low heat for 8–10 minutes, stirring continuously, until the flour is light golden and fragrant. Add the ghee and mix well – the mixture will start to look crumbly.

4 Add the flour mixture to the nut paste along with the agave nectar, cardamom and rose water. Use your hands to combine the mixture well.

5 Take a lime-sized portion of the laddoo mixture in the palm of your hand and compress it into a small ball. Set the laddoo on a serving dish and repeat the shaping process with the remaining mixture.

6 You can serve the laddoos immediately, decorated with dried rose petals, or store them in an airtight container in the refrigerator for 5–6 days. Bring them to room temperature before serving.

Vermicelli Rice Pudding

SERVES 2

500 ml (18 fl oz) whole
  milk
2 tablespoons ghee
30 g (1 oz) cashew
  nuts, roughly
  chopped
30 g (1 oz) blanched
  almonds, roughly
  chopped
30 g (1 oz) raisins – you
  can use a mixture of
  different raisins such
  as black, golden and
  green or just one type
40 g (1 ½ oz) roasted
  vermicelli
40 g (1 ½ oz) light soft
  brown sugar
pinch of ground
  cardamom

When I was little, my grandmother used to make the dough for vermicelli and then spend hours rolling the thin noodles by hand. The noodles would then be left on big steel plates in the sun for days to dry out. My mother has now taken up making vermicelli at home and the last time she came to visit she brought me a big bagful. Vermicelli is now widely available and these days you can buy it ready-roasted, cutting another 5 minutes off your cooking time.

1 Bring the milk to the boil in a pan, then take off the heat and set aside.

2 Heat the ghee in another pan, add the nuts and raisins and cook over a low heat for a minute until they start to change colour.

3 Add the vermicelli and stir well. Then gradually pour in the boiled milk and cook over a low heat for 10 minutes until the vermicelli is just soft.

4 Sprinkle in the sugar and cook for another 5 minutes until the milk is creamy and the vermicelli is cooked through. Then add the cardamom and mix well. Serve warm or at room temperature.

Cardamom and Pistachio Kulfi

SERVES 6

1.5 litres (2¾ pints) milk

50 g (1¾ oz) golden caster sugar

½ teaspoon ground cardamom

3 tablespoons finely chopped pistachio nuts, plus extra to decorate

Kulfi (Indian ice cream) is particularly popular in Delhi, where you find an astonishing variety of flavours these days, from chocolate and mint to paan, yet the traditional combination of cardamom and pistachios remains my favourite. Making kulfi requires patience – no short cuts can give the same amount of flavour as hours spent reducing the milk, so it's definitely worth the effort.

1 Pour the milk into a large, heavy-based saucepan. Bring it to the boil, then reduce the heat to low and simmer for 3 hours, stirring every 5–7 minutes to ensure the milk does not stick to the bottom of the pan.

2 Once the milk has reduced by two-thirds, measure it to ensure the volume has reduced to 500 ml (18 fl oz), then return it to the pan. Add the sugar and cardamom and stir for 1 minute, then add the pistachios. Pour the mixture into a jug and leave it to cool a little.

3 Divide the mixture between 6 kulfi cones (use plastic containers if you don't have any) and freeze overnight.

4 When ready to serve, dip the cones in warm water for a few seconds, then turn out the kulfi onto individual serving plates. Sprinkle with the extra pistachios to serve.

Carrot Halwa

SERVES 6

2 tablespoons ghee
500 g (1 lb 2 oz)
   carrots, peeled and
   grated
500 ml (18 fl oz) milk
50 g (1 ¾ oz)
   granulated sugar
½ teaspoon ground
   cardamom
25 g (1 oz) cashew
   nuts, roughly
   chopped
25 g (1 oz) almonds,
   roughly chopped,
   plus extra to
   decorate
raisins, to decorate

People make this sweet, comforting pudding, known as gajar ka halwa, in winter, when carrots come into season. You'll find it in Delhi and throughout Northern India. People prepare it at home or buy it from street stalls, where the vendors keep the dish warm on large skillets. It is often made with khoya, a thickened milk, but below is a recipe for a slightly lighter version, made with regular milk.

1 Heat the ghee in a wide saucepan over a medium heat. Add the grated carrot and cook for 5 minutes, until it changes colour. Add the milk and bring to a boil. Once the mixture is bubbling, reduce the heat to very low and cook for 40–45 minutes, uncovered, stirring every 5 minutes, until all the milk is absorbed by the carrot.

2 Add the sugar and cardamom to the pan and cook for 5 minutes, until the sugar has melted. Stir in the cashews and almonds. Serve either hot or cold, with the extra almonds and raisins sprinkled on top.

Saffron Barfi

MAKES 12

800 ml (27 fl oz) whole milk
a pinch of saffron
ghee, for greasing
60 g (2¼ oz) granulated sugar
¼ teaspoon ground cardamom
150 g (5½ oz) ground almonds
a handful of pistachio nuts, finely chopped

Barfis can be too sweet but not this delicately flavoured one, which has almonds, bringing an extra dimension of creaminess. It's easy to make but you do need patience, which is well rewarded with a gorgeous pudding.

1 Bring the milk slowly to simmering point in a pan. Add the saffron, reduce the heat to low and cook for 15 minutes, stirring every 2 minutes to prevent sticking.

2 Meanwhile, use some ghee and baking parchment to grease and line a 20 cm (8 inches) square loose-bottomed cake tin.

3 Once the 15 minutes is up, stir the sugar into the milk and cook for 10 minutes, still stirring every 2 minutes. Add the cardamom and almonds and mix well.

4 This is where you need to be patient: continue cooking for 20–25 minutes, stirring slowly the whole time. The mixture will gradually begin to thicken and come together, and will leave the sides of the pan.

5 Quickly tip the mixture into the prepared tin and spread out with a palette knife or the back of a spoon. Sprinkle the pistachios over the barfi and press them in. Leave to set completely. Cut into pieces to serve.

6 You can store this in the refrigerator for 3–4 days – just make sure to leave it at room temperature for about an hour before serving.

Fruit Chaat

SERVES 4

1 banana, peeled and
  roughly chopped
1 apple, cored and
  roughly chopped
seeds from ½
  pomegranate
½ yellow-fleshed
  cantaloupe melon,
  peeled, deseeded and
  roughly chopped
couple of watermelon
  slices, peeled,
  deseeded and
  roughly chopped
1 orange, peeled,
  deseeded and
  roughly chopped
½ teaspoon kala
  namak (black salt)
½ teaspoon chaat
  masala
¼ teaspoon chilli
  flakes
pinch of salt
pinch of freshly
  ground black pepper
2 tablespoons lemon
  juice

Spice up a simple bowl of fruit to make it even more refreshing.
The sour, zingy spices work beautifully with the sweet, crisp
freshness of the fruit. Fruit chaat is a popular Indian street
food, and vendors often vary the spice blend to suit the
combination of fruits. I'm a big fan of this particular combo.

1 Put all the prepared fruits into a bowl, add the spices,
   salt and pepper and lemon juice, then mix well. Serve
   immediately.

Nimbu Paani

SERVES 4
125 ml (4 fl oz) lemon
  juice
juice of 2 limes
4 tablespoons icing
  sugar
½ teaspoon salt
½–¾ teaspoon kala
  namak (black salt)
8 drops of rose water
800 ml (27 fl oz)
  cold water
ice cubes, to serve

Like a rose-scented lemonade, this is one of those refreshing drinks found on every corner of every street in India during the summer. The black salt adds a lovely spicy sourness to the taste of the citrus fruits.

1 Combine the citrus juices in a jug. Add the icing sugar, salts and rose water and mix until the sugar has dissolved. Stir in the measured water.

2 Put some ice into 4 glasses, pour over the nimbu paani and serve.

Mango Lassi

SERVES 3
seeds from 5 green
  cardamom pods
200 g (7 oz) mango
  pulp
200 ml (7 fl oz)
  natural yogurt
100 ml (3½ fl oz) milk
1 tablespoon
  granulated sugar
ice cubes, to serve

I first had this delicious mango lassi in Delhi and, since then,
have always made it at home during mango season. In India,
lassi is considered a hot summer's drink as the ice and yogurt
help you to cool down.

1 Using a pestle and mortar, grind the cardamom seeds to
   a powder.

2 Combine the mango pulp, yogurt, milk, sugar and ground
   cardamom in a blender. Add the ice cubes and blitz for
   1 minute. Pour into 3 glasses and serve immediately.

Masala Chai

300 ml (½ pint) water
1 thick slice of fresh
    root ginger, peeled
    and squashed
2 green cardamom
    pods
2 cloves
2 teaspoons
    granulated sugar
1 tablespoon loose-
    leaf tea or 2 tea bags
5 tablespoons milk

The backbone of Indian street food culture, this drink is available in every nook and cranny of almost every street in India. Everyone has their favourite chai stalls, which they'll visit daily, whether it's day or night. When I was in my final year of college and we were working late at night, a chai walla would come to the gate on a bicycle at around 1am with piping hot chai in a container. All the students who were still up would go and sit in a big group just outside the college to take a break and drink tea together. I learned this masala chai recipe years ago from a tea stall holder in Delhi.

1 Combine the measured water, ginger, cardamom pods and cloves in a saucepan and bring to a boil. Add the sugar and tea, reduce the heat to low and cook for 2 minutes, until the mixture darkens to a deep, strong colour.

2 Stir the milk into the pan and return the mixture to a boil, then reduce the heat and simmer for 2–4 minutes, until well infused.

3 Pass the masala chai carefully through a sieve into 2 cups and serve immediately.

INDEX

A

almonds
  almond halwa 137
  saffron barfi 146
  vermicelli rice pudding 140
Amritsar-style fish 76
apples
  fruit chaat 149
aubergines
  aubergine and
    potato rice 108
  baigan bhaja 22
  tamarind aubergine curry 40

B

baigan bhaja 22
bananas
  fruit chaat 149
basic chapatti 113
beans
  black lentils with red
    kidney beans 98
  mixed vegetable curry 42–3
beetroot, carrot and
  peanut salad 34
Bengali khichdi 106
besan see gram flour
bhakarwadi 16
black lentils with red
  kidney beans 98
black lentils, whole see urad dal
breadcrumbs
  chicken chop 74
  fish chop 27
broccoli
  paneer and purple sprouting
    broccoli sabji 45
bulgur wheat
  tandoori veg kebab 56–7

C

cabbage
  egg and cabbage curry 86
cardamom
  almond halwa 137

Bengali khichdi 106
black lentils with red
  kidney beans 98
cardamom and
  pistachio kulfi 143
mango lassi 152
masala chai 155
onion and whole spice
  chicken curry 68
walnut and hazelnut
  laddoos 138
carrots
  beetroot, carrot and
    peanut salad 34
  carrot and onion pickle 128
  carrot halwa 144
  lentil and mango salad 33
  mixed vegetable curry 42–3
cashew nuts
  korma-style chicken curry 64
  vermicelli rice pudding 140
cauliflower
  cauliflower masala 53
  gobhi 65 20
  mixed vegetable curry 42–3
chana dal
  aubergine and
    potato rice 108
  dal fry 90–1
  dal papdi chaat 24–5
  five lentils 101
chapatti flour
  basic chapatti 113
  gram flour roti 116
  masala puri 120
  walnut and hazelnut
    laddoos 138
cheese
  cheesy potato balls 15
  chicken seekh kebabs 72–3
  crispy paneer cubes 12
  paneer and purple sprouting
    broccoli sabji 45
  potato, paneer and
    chickpea curry 39

tandoori paneer curry 48–9
chicken
  chicken chop 74
  chicken seekh kebabs 72–3
  coconut chicken curry 70
  korma-style chicken curry 64
  masala chicken 62
  onion and whole spice
    chicken curry 68
  whole tandoori-style
    chicken 67
  yogurt chicken curry 60
chickpea flour see gram flour
chickpeas, split see chana dal
chickpeas
  potato, paneer and
    chickpea curry 39
chillies
  Amritsar-style fish 76
  aubergine and
    potato rice 108
  beetroot, carrot and
    peanut salad 34
  Bengali khichdi 106
  black lentils with red
    kidney beans 98
  carrot and onion pickle 128
  cauliflower masala 53
  cheesy potato balls 15
  chicken chop 74
  chicken seekh kebabs 72–3
  coconut chicken curry 70
  coriander and mint
    chutney 132
  cumin dal 92
  dal fry 90–1
  dal papdi chaat 24–5
  fish chop 27
  fish fry 75
  five lentils 101
  garlic and tamarind
    rasam 96
  garlic pickle 125
  hot and spicy coconut
    prawns 84–5

korma-style chicken curry 64
mango and mint chutney 126
mango chutney 124
masala urad dal 93
mixed vegetable curry 42–3
new potato and
    tomato curry 46
onion and whole spice
    chicken curry 68
peanut, coriander and
    lemon rice 105
spinach and coconut dal 95
spinach raita 131
tandoori pan-fried
    sea bream 82
tandoori paneer curry 48–9
ultimate potato sabji 51
coconut
    bhakarwadi 16
    coconut chicken curry 70
    fish and lentil curry 80
    hot and spicy coconut
        prawns 84–5
    spinach and coconut dal 95
    tamarind fish curry 79
cod
    fish chop 27
    tamarind fish curry 79
coriander
    beetroot, carrot and
        peanut salad 34
    Bengali khichdi 106
    black lentils with red
        kidney beans 98
    chicken chop 74
    chicken seekh kebabs 72–3
    coriander and mint
        chutney 132
    cumin dal 92
    cumin rice 104
    dal fry 90–1
    fish fry 75
    korma-style chicken curry 64
    mango and mint
        chutney 126
    masala urad dal 93
    new potato and
        tomato curry 46
    peanut, coriander and
        lemon rice 105
    rava dosa 119

tandoori pan-fried
    sea bream 82
ultimate potato sabji 51
whole tandoori-style
    chicken 67
yogurt chicken curry 60
courgettes
    courgette bharta 36
    tandoori veg kebab 56–7
cream
    egg and cabbage curry 86
    korma-style chicken curry 64
    tandoori paneer curry 48–9
crispy paneer cubes 12
cucumber
    lentil and mango salad 33
cumin dal 92
cumin rice 104

D
dahi puri 10
dal fry 90–1
dal papdi chaat 24–5
dates
    tamarind and date
        chutney 133

E
eggs
    chicken chop 74
    egg and cabbage curry 86
    fish chop 27

F
fennel seeds
    bhakarwadi 16
    cauliflower masala 53
    hot and spicy coconut
        prawns 84–5
    tamarind and date
        chutney 133
    tamarind aubergine curry 40
fish
    Amritsar-style fish 76
    fish and lentil curry 80
    fish chop 27
    fish fry 75
    tamarind fish curry 79
    tandoori pan-fried
        sea bream 82
five lentils 101

flatbreads
    basic chapatti 113
    gram flour roti 116
    masala puri 120
    parotha 114–15
    quick naan 112
    rava dosa 119
fruit chaat 149

G
garlic
    garlic and tamarind
        rasam 96
    garlic pickle 125
    garlicky mushroom sabji 44
gobhi 65 20
gram flour
    baigan bhaji 22
    cheesy potato balls 15
    crispy paneer cubes 12
    gram flour roti 116

H
hake
    fish and lentil curry 80
hazelnuts
    walnut and hazelnut
        laddoos 138
hot and spicy coconut
    prawns 84–5

J
jaggery
    garlic pickle 125
    tamarind and date
        chutney 133

K
korma-style chicken curry 64

L
lemons
    fish fry 75
    nimbu paani 150
    peanut, coriander and
        lemon rice 105
    sour and spicy okra
        with potatoes 54
    tandoori veg kebab 56–7
    whole tandoori-style
        chicken 67

lentils
    black lentils with red
        kidney beans 98
    fish and lentil curry 80
    five lentils 101
    lentil and mango salad 33
limes
    Amritsar-style fish 76
    beetroot, carrot and
        peanut salad 34
    chicken seekh kebabs 72–3
    coriander and mint
        chutney 132
    courgette bharta 36
    mango and mint
        chutney 126
    new potato and
        tomato curry 46
    nimbu paani 150
    tandoori pan-fried
        sea bream 82

M
mango
    lentil and mango salad 33
    mango and mint
        chutney 126
    mango chutney 124
    mango lassi 152
masala chai 155
masala chicken 62
masala papdi 28
masala peanuts 29
masala puri 120
masala urad dal 93
melon
    fruit chaat 149
milk
    almond halwa 137
    cardamom and
        pistachio kulfi 143
    mango lassi 152
    masala chai 155
    parotha 114–15
    saffron barfi 146
    vermicelli rice pudding 140
mint
    cauliflower masala 53
    mango and mint
        chutney 126
mixed vegetable curry 42–3

moong dal
    Bengali khichdi 106
    cumin dal 92
    dal fry 90–1
    five lentils 101
    lentil and mango salad 33
mung beans, split see
    moong dal
mushrooms
    garlicky mushroom sabji 44

N
naan, quick 112
new potato and
    tomato curry 46
nimbu paani 150

O
okra
    sour and spicy okra
        with potatoes 54
onions
    Amritsar-style fish 76
    aubergine and
        potato rice 108
    beetroot, carrot and
        peanut salad 34
    carrot and onion pickle 128
    cauliflower masala 53
    chicken chop 74
    chicken seekh kebabs 72–3
    coconut chicken curry 70
    dal fry 90–1
    egg and cabbage curry 86
    fish and lentil curry 80
    fish chop 27
    five lentils 101
    garlicky mushroom sabji 44
    hot and spicy coconut
        prawns 84–5
    korma-style chicken curry 64
    lentil and mango salad 33
    masala urad dal 93
    mixed vegetable curry 42–3
    onion and whole spice
        chicken curry 68
    paneer and purple sprouting
        broccoli sabji 45
    peanut, coriander and
        lemon rice 105
    rava dosa 119

sour and spicy okra
    with potatoes 54
tamarind aubergine curry 40
tandoori paneer curry 48–9
tandoori veg kebab 56–7
ultimate potato sabji 51
vegetable pulao 111
oranges
    fruit chaat 149

P
paneer
    crispy paneer cubes 12
    paneer and purple sprouting
        broccoli sabji 45
    potato, paneer and
        chickpea curry 39
    tandoori paneer curry 48–9
parotha 114–15
pastries
    bhakarwadi 16
    masala papdi 28
peanuts
    beetroot, carrot and
        peanut salad 34
    masala peanuts 29
    peanut, coriander and
        lemon rice 105
peas
    vegetable pulao 111
peppers
    vegetable pulao 111
pigeon peas, split see toor dal
pistachios
    almond halwa 137
    cardamom and
        pistachio kulfi 143
    saffron barfi 146
plain flour
    bhakarwadi 16
    dal papdi chaat 24–5
    masala papdi 28
    parotha 114–15
pomegranates
    fruit chaat 149
poppy seeds
    bhakarwadi 16
    korma-style chicken curry 64
potatoes
    aubergine and potato rice 108
    cheesy potato balls 15

chicken chop 74
dahi puri
new potato and
tomato curry 46
potato, paneer and
chickpea curry 39
smashed alu tikki 19
sour and spicy okra
with potatoes 54
ultimate potato sabji 51
prawns
hot and spicy coconut
prawns 84–5
puris
dahi puri 10
masala puri 120

R
raisins
vermicelli rice pudding 140
rava dosa 119
rice
aubergine and
potato rice 108
Bengali khichdi 106
cumin rice 104
peanut, coriander and
lemon rice 105
vegetable pulao 111
vermicelli rice pudding 140
rose water
nimbu paani 150
walnut and hazelnut
laddoos 138

S
saffron
almond halwa 137
saffron barfi 146
sea bream
fish fry 75
tandoori pan-fried
sea bream 82
self-raising flour
quick naan 112
semolina
rava dosa 119
sesame seeds
bhakarwadi 16
new potato and
tomato curry 46

shallots
tamarind fish curry 79
smashed alu tikki 19
sour and spicy okra
with potatoes 54
spices
onion and whole spice
chicken curry 68
spinach and coconut dal 95
spinach raita 131
spring onions
vegetable pulao 111
sweet potatoes
tandoori veg kebab 56–7

T
tamarind
garlic and tamarind rasam 96
tamarind and date chutney 133
tamarind aubergine curry 40
tamarind fish curry 79
tandoori pan-fried
sea bream 82
tandoori paneer curry 48–9
tandoori veg kebab 56–7
tea
masala chai 155
tomatoes
Bengali khichdi 106
black lentils with red
kidney beans 98
cauliflower masala 53
fish and lentil curry 80
five lentils 101
masala urad dal 93
mixed vegetable curry 42–3
new potato and
tomato curry 46
onion and whole spice
chicken curry 68
potato, paneer and
chickpea curry 39
sour and spicy okra
with potatoes 54
tandoori paneer curry 48–9
vegetable pulao 111
yogurt chicken curry 60
toor dal
dal fry 90–1
five lentils 101
spinach and coconut dal 95

trout
Amritsar-style fish 76

U
ultimate potato sabji 51
urad dal
aubergine and
potato rice 108
black lentils with red
kidney beans 98
five lentils 101
masala urad dal 93

V
vegetables
mixed vegetable curry 42–3
tandoori veg kebab 56–7
vegetable pulao 111
vermicelli rice pudding 140

W
walnut and hazelnut
laddoos 138
watermelon
fruit chaat 149
whole tandoori-style
chicken 67

Y
yogurt
chicken seekh kebabs 72–3
crispy paneer cubes 12
dahi puri 10
garlicky mushroom sabji 44
mango lassi 152
masala chicken 62
onion and whole spice
chicken curry 68
quick naan 112
rava dosa 119
smashed alu tikki 19
spinach raita 131
tandoori pan-fried
sea bream 82
tandoori veg kebab 56–7
whole tandoori-style
chicken 67
yogurt chicken curry 60

GLOSSARY OF TERMS

UK	US
aubergine	eggplant
baking tray	baking sheet
barbecue	grill
beetroot	beets
cake tin	cake pan
caster sugar	superfine sugar
chickpeas	garbanzo beans
chilli/chillies	chili/chiles
chilli flakes	red pepper flakes
clingfilm	plastic wrap
coriander (fresh)	cilantro
cornflour	cornstarch
courgette	zucchini
desiccated coconut	unsweetened desiccated coconut
double cream	heavy cream
frying pan	skillet
gram flour	besan/chickpea flour
green pepper	green bell pepper
grill	broil/broiler
groundnut oil	peanut oil
hob	stove
icing sugar	confectioners' sugar
jug	pitcher
kitchen paper	paper towels
plain flour	all-purpose flour
rapeseed oil	canola oil
self-raising flour	self-rising flour
shops	stores
sieve	strainer
spring onions	scallions
Swiss roll	jelly roll
tea towel	dishtowel
tomato purée	tomato paste

korma-style chicken curry 64
mango and mint chutney 126
mango chutney 124
masala urad dal 93
mixed vegetable curry 42–3
new potato and
    tomato curry 46
onion and whole spice
    chicken curry 68
peanut, coriander and
    lemon rice 105
spinach and coconut dal 95
spinach raita 131
tandoori pan-fried
    sea bream 82
tandoori paneer curry 48–9
ultimate potato sabji 51
coconut
    bhakarwadi 16
    coconut chicken curry 70
    fish and lentil curry 80
    hot and spicy coconut
        prawns 84–5
    spinach and coconut dal 95
    tamarind fish curry 79
cod
    fish chop 27
    tamarind fish curry 79
coriander
    beetroot, carrot and
        peanut salad 34
    Bengali khichdi 106
    black lentils with red
        kidney beans 98
    chicken chop 74
    chicken seekh kebabs 72–3
    coriander and mint
        chutney 132
    cumin dal 92
    cumin rice 104
    dal fry 90–1
    fish fry 75
    korma-style chicken curry 64
    mango and mint
        chutney 126
    masala urad dal 93
    new potato and
        tomato curry 46
    peanut, coriander and
        lemon rice 105
    rava dosa 119

tandoori pan-fried
    sea bream 82
ultimate potato sabji 51
whole tandoori-style
    chicken 67
yogurt chicken curry 60
courgettes
    courgette bharta 36
    tandoori veg kebab 56–7
cream
    egg and cabbage curry 86
    korma-style chicken curry 64
    tandoori paneer curry 48–9
crispy paneer cubes 12
cucumber
    lentil and mango salad 33
cumin dal 92
cumin rice 104

D
dahi puri 10
dal fry 90–1
dal papdi chaat 24–5
dates
    tamarind and date
        chutney 133

E
eggs
    chicken chop 74
    egg and cabbage curry 86
    fish chop 27

F
fennel seeds
    bhakarwadi 16
    cauliflower masala 53
    hot and spicy coconut
        prawns 84–5
    tamarind and date
        chutney 133
    tamarind aubergine curry 40
fish
    Amritsar-style fish 76
    fish and lentil curry 80
    fish chop 27
    fish fry 75
    tamarind fish curry 79
    tandoori pan-fried
        sea bream 82
five lentils 101

flatbreads
    basic chapatti 113
    gram flour roti 116
    masala puri 120
    parotha 114–15
    quick naan 112
    rava dosa 119
fruit chaat 149

G
garlic
    garlic and tamarind
        rasam 96
    garlic pickle 125
    garlicky mushroom sabji 44
gobhi 65 20
gram flour
    baigan bhaji 22
    cheesy potato balls 15
    crispy paneer cubes 12
    gram flour roti 116

H
hake
    fish and lentil curry 80
hazelnuts
    walnut and hazelnut
        laddoos 138
hot and spicy coconut
    prawns 84–5

J
jaggery
    garlic pickle 125
    tamarind and date
        chutney 133

K
korma-style chicken curry 64

L
lemons
    fish fry 75
    nimbu paani 150
    peanut, coriander and
        lemon rice 105
    sour and spicy okra
        with potatoes 54
    tandoori veg kebab 56–7
    whole tandoori-style
        chicken 67

lentils
    black lentils with red
        kidney beans 98
    fish and lentil curry 80
    five lentils 101
    lentil and mango salad 33
limes
    Amritsar-style fish 76
    beetroot, carrot and
        peanut salad 34
    chicken seekh kebabs 72–3
    coriander and mint
        chutney 132
    courgette bharta 36
    mango and mint
        chutney 126
    new potato and
        tomato curry 46
    nimbu paani 150
    tandoori pan-fried
        sea bream 82

M

mango
    lentil and mango salad 33
    mango and mint
        chutney 126
    mango chutney 124
    mango lassi 152
masala chai 155
masala chicken 62
masala papdi 28
masala peanuts 29
masala puri 120
masala urad dal 93
melon
    fruit chaat 149
milk
    almond halwa 137
    cardamom and
        pistachio kulfi 143
    mango lassi 152
    masala chai 155
    parotha 114–15
    saffron barfi 146
    vermicelli rice pudding 140
mint
    cauliflower masala 53
    mango and mint
        chutney 126
mixed vegetable curry 42–3

moong dal
    Bengali khichdi 106
    cumin dal 92
    dal fry 90–1
    five lentils 101
    lentil and mango salad 33
mung beans, split *see*
    moong dal
mushrooms
    garlicky mushroom sabji 44

N

naan, quick 112
new potato and
    tomato curry 46
nimbu paani 150

O

okra
    sour and spicy okra
        with potatoes 54
onions
    Amritsar-style fish 76
    aubergine and
        potato rice 108
    beetroot, carrot and
        peanut salad 34
    carrot and onion pickle 128
    cauliflower masala 53
    chicken chop 74
    chicken seekh kebabs 72–3
    coconut chicken curry 70
    dal fry 90–1
    egg and cabbage curry 86
    fish and lentil curry 80
    fish chop 27
    five lentils 101
    garlicky mushroom sabji 44
    hot and spicy coconut
        prawns 84–5
    korma-style chicken curry 64
    lentil and mango salad 33
    masala urad dal 93
    mixed vegetable curry 42–3
    onion and whole spice
        chicken curry 68
    paneer and purple sprouting
        broccoli sabji 45
    peanut, coriander and
        lemon rice 105
    rava dosa 119

sour and spicy okra
    with potatoes 54
tamarind aubergine curry 40
tandoori paneer curry 48–9
tandoori veg kebab 56–7
ultimate potato sabji 51
vegetable pulao 111
oranges
    fruit chaat 149

P

paneer
    crispy paneer cubes 12
    paneer and purple sprouting
        broccoli sabji 45
    potato, paneer and
        chickpea curry 39
    tandoori paneer curry 48–9
parotha 114–15
pastries
    bhakarwadi 16
    masala papdi 28
peanuts
    beetroot, carrot and
        peanut salad 34
    masala peanuts 29
    peanut, coriander and
        lemon rice 105
peas
    vegetable pulao 111
peppers
    vegetable pulao 111
pigeon peas, split *see* toor dal
pistachios
    almond halwa 137
    cardamom and
        pistachio kulfi 143
    saffron barfi 146
plain flour
    bhakarwadi 16
    dal papdi chaat 24–5
    masala papdi 28
    parotha 114–15
pomegranates
    fruit chaat 149
poppy seeds
    bhakarwadi 16
    korma-style chicken curry 64
potatoes
    aubergine and potato rice 108
    cheesy potato balls 15

chicken chop 74
dahi puri
new potato and
 tomato curry 46
potato, paneer and
 chickpea curry 39
smashed alu tikki 19
sour and spicy okra
 with potatoes 54
ultimate potato sabji 51
prawns
 hot and spicy coconut
  prawns 84–5
puris
 dahi puri 10
 masala puri 120

R
raisins
 vermicelli rice pudding 140
rava dosa 119
rice
 aubergine and
  potato rice 108
 Bengali khichdi 106
 cumin rice 104
 peanut, coriander and
  lemon rice 105
 vegetable pulao 111
 vermicelli rice pudding 140
rose water
 nimbu paani 150
 walnut and hazelnut
  laddoos 138

S
saffron
 almond halwa 137
 saffron barfi 146
sea bream
 fish fry 75
 tandoori pan-fried
  sea bream 82
self-raising flour
 quick naan 112
semolina
 rava dosa 119
sesame seeds
 bhakarwadi 16
 new potato and
  tomato curry 46

shallots
 tamarind fish curry 79
smashed alu tikki 19
sour and spicy okra
 with potatoes 54
spices
 onion and whole spice
  chicken curry 68
spinach and coconut dal 95
spinach raita 131
spring onions
 vegetable pulao 111
sweet potatoes
 tandoori veg kebab 56–7

T
tamarind
 garlic and tamarind rasam 96
 tamarind and date chutney 133
 tamarind aubergine curry 40
 tamarind fish curry 79
tandoori pan-fried
 sea bream 82
tandoori paneer curry 48–9
tandoori veg kebab 56–7
tea
 masala chai 155
tomatoes
 Bengali khichdi 106
 black lentils with red
  kidney beans 98
 cauliflower masala 53
 fish and lentil curry 80
 five lentils 101
 masala urad dal 93
 mixed vegetable curry 42–3
 new potato and
  tomato curry 46
 onion and whole spice
  chicken curry 68
 potato, paneer and
  chickpea curry 39
 sour and spicy okra
  with potatoes 54
 tandoori paneer curry 48–9
 vegetable pulao 111
 yogurt chicken curry 60
toor dal
 dal fry 90–1
 five lentils 101
 spinach and coconut dal 95

trout
 Amritsar-style fish 76

U
ultimate potato sabji 51
urad dal
 aubergine and
  potato rice 108
 black lentils with red
  kidney beans 98
 five lentils 101
 masala urad dal 93

V
vegetables
 mixed vegetable curry 42–3
 tandoori veg kebab 56–7
 vegetable pulao 111
vermicelli rice pudding 140

W
walnut and hazelnut
 laddoos 138
watermelon
 fruit chaat 149
whole tandoori-style
 chicken 67

Y
yogurt
 chicken seekh kebabs 72–3
 crispy paneer cubes 12
 dahi puri 10
 garlicky mushroom sabji 44
 mango lassi 152
 masala chicken 62
 onion and whole spice
  chicken curry 68
 quick naan 112
 rava dosa 119
 smashed alu tikki 19
 spinach raita 131
 tandoori pan-fried
  sea bream 82
 tandoori veg kebab 56–7
 whole tandoori-style
  chicken 67
 yogurt chicken curry 60

GLOSSARY OF TERMS

UK	US
aubergine	eggplant
baking tray	baking sheet
barbecue	grill
beetroot	beets
cake tin	cake pan
caster sugar	superfine sugar
chickpeas	garbanzo beans
chilli/chillies	chili/chiles
chilli flakes	red pepper flakes
clingfilm	plastic wrap
coriander (fresh)	cilantro
cornflour	cornstarch
courgette	zucchini
desiccated coconut	unsweetened desiccated coconut
double cream	heavy cream
frying pan	skillet
gram flour	besan/chickpea flour
green pepper	green bell pepper
grill	broil/broiler
groundnut oil	peanut oil
hob	stove
icing sugar	confectioners' sugar
jug	pitcher
kitchen paper	paper towels
plain flour	all-purpose flour
rapeseed oil	canola oil
self-raising flour	self-rising flour
shops	stores
sieve	strainer
spring onions	scallions
Swiss roll	jelly roll
tea towel	dishtowel
tomato purée	tomato paste